Pubs and Places:

The social value of community pu

Rick Muir

Contents

Institute for Public Policy Research

About ippr

The Institute for Public Policy Research is the UK's leading progressive think tank, producing cutting-edge research and innovative policy ideas for a just, democratic and sustainable world.

Since 1988, we have been at the forefront of progressive debate and policymaking in the UK. Through our independent research and analysis we define new agendas for change and provide practical solutions to challenges across the full range of public policy issues.

With offices in both London and Newcastle, we ensure our outlook is as broad-based as possible, while our international and migration teams and climate change programme extend our partnerships and influence beyond the UK, giving us a truly world-class reputation for high quality research.

About the author

Rick Muir is a Senior Research Fellow at the Institute for Public Policy Research. His research focuses on communities, politics and public services. His previous publications for ippr include *The Power of Belonging: Identity, citizenship and community cohesion* (with Ben Rogers), *A New Beat: Options for more accountable policing* (with Guy Lodge) and *Sticking Together: Social capital and local government* (ed. with Halima Kahn). He has a doctorate in Politics from Oxford University, where he taught and lectured on Latin American politics.

Acknowledgements

ippr would like to thank the Campaign for Real Ale (CAMRA) for their generous support of this project.

The author would like to thank all those who contributed to his thinking during the course of the research, in particular Guy Lodge, Mike Benner, Jonathan Mail, Michael Kenny, Gill Gibson, Ruth Sheldon, Naomi Jones, Matthew Lockwood, Tony Dolphin, Karl Hallam, John Pritchard, John Grogan MP and Greg Mulholland MP. Thanks to all those pub regulars and licensees who took the time to talk to me during the course of the research. Thanks, too, go to Georgina Kyriacou for her help in bringing this report to print.

Any omissions and errors remain the author's, and the report's analysis and recommendations do not necessarily represent the views of the project's supporters.

Executive summary

Community pubs are one of Britain's oldest and most popular social institutions. However, they are currently under pressure, with 39 pubs now closing every week. This report assesses the social value of community pubs, showing why pubs matter and why we should be concerned about the current state of the pub trade.

An audit of Britain's community pubs

This report's audit of community pubs shows that their numbers have been falling gradually for decades, but that closure rates have accelerated in the last two years.

Why are so many pubs closing? A number of connected factors have all played a role:

- Alcohol consumption tends to rise and fall with economic prosperity and the recent downturn in the economy has affected pub incomes.
- Many of the old industrial and village communities surrounding local pubs have changed out of all recognition, reducing the number of devoted pub regulars in some areas.
- Tastes and lifestyles have changed with more people drinking wine and fewer people drinking beer, the mainstay of most pub income. The pub has faced competition from alternative leisure pursuits, such as the restaurant and the cinema. There has also been a significant rise in the number of people drinking at home, rather than in pubs and bars.
- Beer prices have gone up in pubs and bars much faster than in shops and supermarkets and supermarket discounts are thought to be one of the major factors in falling pub incomes.
- Pub operators have faced rising costs as beer prices have increased and major legislative changes have imposed significant additional costs.
- There is evidence that tenants of some of the large pub companies are finding it hard to compete because of the higher prices they are paying for their tied beer. There is also a lack of transparency in the way some pub companies calculate their rents.

Why do pubs matter?

Pubs are more than just private businesses selling alcohol – very many pubs also play an important role at the heart of their local communities:

- Pubs provide a meeting place where social networks are strengthened and extended: the pub scored the highest of any location in our survey asking people where they get together with others in their neighbourhood.
- Pubs inject an average of £80,000 into their local economy each year. Pubs add more value to local economies than beer sold through shops and supermarkets, simply because they generate more jobs. Beer sold through

pubs also generates more funding for the public purse than beer sold through the 'off trade'.
• While alcohol is linked to problems around crime and disorder, very little of this comes from community pubs serving residential areas.
• Pubs are perceived by people to be the most important social institution for promoting interactions between people from different walks of life.
• Pubs host a wide variety of community oriented events and activities that add considerably to local civic life.
• Many community pubs are becoming hosts for a range of important public services, including post offices and general stores and providing broadband internet access.
• Community pubs, or at least pubs with certain characteristics, also have a cultural as well as a practical community value. This is because pubs are felt to offer things such as tradition and authenticity that are becoming rarer in a world transformed by global commercial pressures.

Time for change

The current policy framework regarding community pubs contains three major flaws:

• It is far too indiscriminate: all licensed premises have to carry the burden of new regulations and increased taxation, but the smaller community pubs that cause so few of the problems are those least able to take on these additional costs. We need a more nuanced approach that targets the problem drinking places and rewards and incentivises pubs that play a positive role in their local communities.
• It is counter-productive, particularly in terms of tackling crime and disorder: by making beer in pubs more expensive while beer in shops and supermarkets gets relatively cheaper, policy is drawing people out of the regulated and supervised drinking environment of the pub.
• Policy fails to recognise that very many pubs are more than just businesses and perform important community functions which if lost can have a serious impact on the quality of local community life.

Recommendations

To provide greater support to the majority of well-run community pubs, ippr recommends:

• **Business rate relief for 'centres of community'**: where pubs act as local community hubs they should be granted 50 per cent mandatory business rate relief. We have produced a method for measuring the social impact of a community pub which could be used to determine which pubs should qualify.
• **Eligibility for third sector finance**: some pubs could apply to become Community Interest Companies and apply for third sector grants and loans to develop the community-oriented side of their business.

- **Reform of planning law:** to provide greater protection for community pubs. In the absence of nationwide reform, local authorities should use the Sustainable Communities Act to help them safeguard pubs as important local amenities.
- **Buying pubs:** existing tenants should be given the first option of buying their pub if it is put up for sale.
- **A minimum price for a unit of alcohol:** to prevent irresponsible promotions and close the gap between the on and the off trades, a minimum price should be introduced.
- **Beer duty:** there should be no further increases in beer duty at a time of escalating pub closures. The Government should abandon its current 'beer duty escalator'.
- **The relationship between the large pub companies and their tenants:** this relationship needs to be rebalanced. The way the beer tie is currently operated needs to be reformed and a mandatory code of conduct should be introduced to ensure that rents are calculated in a transparent way and that there is an independent and accessible arbitration system to settle disputes between pubcos and their tenants.
- **Diversification:** pubs themselves need to diversify what they offer and keep pace with consumer tastes and demand.
- **Training and development:** the pub trade needs to develop a stronger culture of training and professional development.

There is no one magic bullet that will simultaneously solve the problems facing Britain's community pubs. However, taken as a whole, the package of measures recommended here should ensure that local pubs can continue to play a role in supporting community life for many generations to come.

1. Introduction

There are few institutions so central to Britain's culture and way of life as the local public house. Try to imagine *Coronation Street* without The Rover's Return, *Emmerdale* without The Woolpack or *EastEnders* without The Queen Vic. Outside the home the pub is the most popular place for British people of all ages and classes to relax and socialise.

And yet pubs are under pressure. Some of this pressure is economic in nature: many pubs are closing, having been caught in a dangerous cross fire between changing consumer tastes, intense supermarket competition and the current recession.

Pubs have also come under political pressure because of concerns about rising levels of alcohol consumption and the impact that has had on levels of crime and disorder: we are all familiar with the scenes of so-called binge-drinking in our town centres on a Friday and Saturday night. There are also concerns about the impact of excessive alcohol consumption on people's health and tackling this is one of the motivations for increasing alcohol duties.

The vast majority of community pubs are well run and contribute in a positive way to local social life. Despite this the policy instruments used to suppress excessive drinking have put financial pressure on local community pubs right across the country. This report argues that we need a more nuanced approach.

The report does three things:

- It audits the health of the community pub trade in the UK and concludes that pub numbers have been in decline for decades, with closure rates accelerating in the last two years. It then goes on to explain why so many pubs have closed, discussing the impact of the wider economy, changing consumer tastes, government policy and the ownership structure within the pub trade.
- It sets out why community pubs matter and why we should be concerned about the number of pubs that are closing.
- It makes the case for a more active role for government and other actors in supporting community pubs and recommends a number of policy changes that should help secure the future of Britain's community pubs in the years ahead.

Before going on to explore the current challenges pubs face, this introductory chapter helps to frame what follows by defining what a community pub is, describing the current composition of the pub trade and outlining how we conducted our research.

What is a community pub?

A 'community pub' is not easy to define, largely because there is no such thing as a typical British pub and, if anything, the range of bars and drinking establishments has become more varied in recent years (Fox 1996, Jennings 2007). People often make a distinction between pubs and bars, for example, and few people describe large city centre circuit bars as pubs.

The concept of the pub is a fuzzy one, a constellation of popular understandings of what a typical pub looks like that has evolved over time. In one of the earliest anthropological studies of the British pub, undertaken in Bolton in the 1930s, Mass Observation concluded that 'the pub, reduced to its lowest terms, is a house where during certain hours everyone is free to buy and drink a glass of beer' (Mass Observation 1943: 17). Ben Davis builds on this by emphasising the social orientation of the drinking that occurs in a pub, which is definitive of it: 'A pub is a house open to the public at stated times for the purpose of social drinking. Any other purpose, such as eating or entertainment, is incidental' (Davis 1981: 2).

Box 1.1. A breakdown of the 140,000 on-licensed premises in the UK

- **Town centre pubs, bars and clubs:** 16 per cent (22,000)
  An outlet in a town/city centre location on a 'circuit'. Many are owned by chains such as O'Neills, Wetherspoons, Yates's Wine Lodge.

- **Food-led pubs:** 7 per cent (10,000)
  An outlet with a recognised retail brand, with food as the primary focus. For example, Beefeater, Harvester and Brewers Fayre. This also includes pubs in which the sale of food is significant to overall sales.

- **Local/community:** 57 per cent (40,000)
  Pubs that serve predominantly their local residential community. This includes pubs in many different types of area, including inner city pubs, village pubs, and estate pubs, and aimed at different clienteles, such as family pubs, student pubs, sports pubs and music pubs (Fox 1996).

- **Licensed accommodation:** 11 per cent (15,000)
  A mixture of businesses whose focus is an overnight stay or short breaks or holidays.

- **Licensed restaurants:** 15 per cent (21,000)
  Restaurants with a licence to sell alcoholic beverages with meals.

- **Sports, social and members clubs:** 23 per cent (32,000)
  Clubs that are licensed and operated for the benefit primarily of their membership.

Source: CGA Strategy Drinks 2009a

In this report we are concerned specifically with community pubs, which market researchers CGA Strategy define as 'pubs that serve predominately their local residential community'. These pubs make up 57 per cent of the total licensed 'on-trade' in the UK (CGA Strategy 2009). These can be distinguished from town centre bars which largely serve after-work or weekend drinkers and which have been the focus of concerns about 'binge drinking' in recent years. Community pubs can also be distinguished from food-led pubs, which people visit predominantly to have a meal rather than to drink (see Box 1.1 for the CGA drinks places typology).

Community pubs have two distinct but intrinsically related functions. One is as a retail outlet to sell alcoholic drinks and the other is as a place for social interaction (Boston 1975). The drink and the socialising of course go hand in hand: after a few alcoholic drinks, the often random social encounters that occur in pubs become much easier as people shed their inhibitions. A pub without drink would not be a pub.

At the same time, pubs are not just about beer: if everyone visited a pub to drink alcohol on their own, a definitive component of pub culture would be lost. The community pub at its heart is an institution for social drinking and it is from fulfilling that function that so many of its positive benefits flow.

The changing composition of the pub trade
Community pubs operate under many different forms of ownership and management, ranging from independent free houses to pubs owned by large pub companies or 'pubcos'. The whole way in which pubs are owned and run has changed significantly in the last twenty years and, before we move on, it is worth recounting the story of how that change came about.

Over the course of the last century the number of breweries in Britain fell from 6,290 to just 115 by 1989 (Haydon 1994). By the end of the 1980s over 75 per cent of Britain's beer was produced by just six large brewers: Bass Charrington, Allied, Whitbread, Watney Mann, Courage and Scottish and Newcastle. These national brewers also owned half of the country's pubs, meaning that most pubs were 'tied' to a big brewer and could only sell that brewer's beer (Jennings 2007).

In 1989 the Monopolies and Mergers Commission (MMC) concluded that this vertical integration of the industry with the big brewers controlling most of the pubs constituted a monopoly which reduced consumer choice and operated against the public interest. It proposed that the brewers' monopoly over the pub estate should be broken up so to encourage competition and reduce retail prices.

Margaret Thatcher, who of course hated monopolies, backed the MMC's recommendations and passed the 1989 Beer Orders. These meant that brewers owning any more than 2,000 pubs either had to sell their brewery business or dispose or free from tie half of the number of pubs over 2,000 that they owned (Jennings 2007, Kingsnorth 2008).

This was a revolutionary act that transformed the structure of the pub trade, but did not have the consequences anticipated by the Government. Instead of leading to a world of independent licensees free of beer ties, the brewers divested their pub estate to stand-alone pub companies, who were free to own as many pubs as they wanted because they did not brew their own beer. The pubs formerly owned by the brewers were almost entirely put into the hands of the new pub companies (see Table 1.1).

By 2004, pubcos owned 57 per cent of the pubs in the UK, with the six largest pubcos owning 40 per cent and with Enterprise Inns and Punch Taverns owning 30 per cent between them (Trade and Industry Select Committee 2004). Of the remaining pub stock 14 per cent are owned by small or regional brewers and 28 per cent are free houses.

In most cases the pubcos let out their pubs to tenants who run their own business, although around 10,000 are managed directly by the pubco. In addition to paying rent, pubco tenants normally have to purchase almost all of their drink from the pubco. This relationship has become increasingly fraught as economic conditions have worsened and pubco beer prices have increased. It has become apparent to many licensees that they could buy their beer more cheaply on the free market if they were able to do so.

It is worth emphasising that the bulk of these pubco pubs are community pubs, serving local residential areas, although some will also be town and city centre circuit bars or branded chain pubs. Our focus in this report is on community pubs of all kinds, whether free houses or owned and/or managed by a pubco or brewer.

Table 1.1. Ownership of UK pubs by type of operator, for years 1989 and 2004		
Ownership type	1989	2004
National brewers		
Tenants/leased	22,000	0
Managed	10,000	0
Subtotal	32,000	0
Regional brewers		
Tenants/leased	9,000	5,972
Managed	3,000	2,617
Subtotal	12,000	8,589
Independents		
Tenants/leased	Negligible	23,857
Managed	Negligible	10,268
Freehouses	16,000	16,850
Subtotal	16,000	50,975
Total	60,000	59,564
Source: House of Commons Trade and Industry Select Committee (2004: 8)		

| Table 1.2. Estimated number of public houses owned by large pubcos, 2008 ||
Pubco	Number of pubs
Punch Taverns	8,524
Enterprise Inns	7,783
Admiral Taverns	2,700
Mitchell & Butlers	1,892
County Estate Management	950
Wellington Pub Company	855
JD Weatherspoon PLC	690
Trust Inns	602
Source: British Beer and Pub Association 2008: 103-105	

ippr's research

There were five main components to the research:

- A review of the literature on the British public house, including work on the history of the pub and anthropological studies of pub behaviour.

- A national omnibus poll of 1,057 people which gauged public attitudes to the pub and tested its importance to community life. This poll took place from 7 to 11 January 2009.

- Twenty interviews with pub licensees from around the country to understand the pressures they are under and the role their pubs play in their local communities. These were licensees from a mixture of rural and urban pubs and from free houses, managed houses and tenanted houses (whether owned by a pub company or a brewer). This sample was chosen from a selection of pubs recommended by the Campaign for Real Ale and highlighted by the Pub is the Hub organisation, plus half were randomly selected by the author (see Appendix A). It could not and is not intended to be a nationally representative sample.

- Three focus groups with pub regulars, selected on site by the author or by recommendation of the licensee.

  The aim of the groups was to explore in detail with pub regulars their motivation for frequenting their local pub and what they got out of it. These were all wet-led – that is, earning most of their income from drinks – community pubs serving a local residential community. They included an urban pub situated in Hackney, East London, whose main clientele comes from a neighbouring council estate. Another was a rural pub, one of a number serving a Hertfordshire town and its surrounding area. The final group took place in a village pub in Cambridgeshire, which was the single remaining pub in the village. The Hackney and Hertfordshire groups took place on Wednesday evenings in December 2008 and January 2009 respectively. The Cambridgeshire group took place on a Friday lunch time in January 2009.

The focus groups were all held in the pubs themselves. Appendix B sets out the details of each group and some characteristics of the participants. The overwhelming majority of the pub regulars recruited were male and middle-aged, simply because these were the regular pub goers encountered on site or recommended by licensees. The objective behind the focus group research was not to question a representative sample of the pub-going population; rather, it was to understand in greater depth the motivations and experiences of a selection of regular pub goers.

- A roundtable seminar held at ippr (London) on 25 February 2009 at which we presented our preliminary research findings, attended by a wide range of stakeholders from across the pub trade, as well as policymakers, academics and independent commentators. The Sports Minister Gerry Sutcliffe MP and the Chief Executive of the Campaign for Real Ale Mike Benner responded to the presentation.

2. Last chance saloon? An audit of Britain's community pubs

'When you have lost your inns, drown your empty selves, for you will have lost the last of England.' **Hilaire Belloc (1948)**

Pub closures

The British pub trade is in trouble. In total 1,973 pubs closed in 2008, up from 1,409 in 2007. That amounts to 39 pubs a week closing in the last six months of 2008, up from 36 pubs a week in the first half of that year and just four a week in 2006 (British Beer and Pub Association [BBPA] 2009).

Community pubs serving their local residential community have been hit the hardest. Suburban pub closures in the last six months of 2008 were running at 19 a week, compared to eight a week for town-centre pubs and 13 a week for rural pubs (BBPA 2009). While few might mourn the loss of large city-centre circuit bars, suburban and village pubs provide a whole range of social and community benefits that are put at risk whenever such pubs fail.

These figures showing rising pub closures would not be so alarming if the rate of new pubs opening was keeping pace. However, the evidence is that the overall number of pubs in the country is falling: between 2005 and 2009 the number of pubs in England, Scotland and Wales fell by 4,271 (CGA Strategy 2009b).

This is not just a phenomenon of the last few years, but has been ongoing for well over a century. As Mass Observation noted, in the 1930s: 'The pub today plays a smaller part in the life of the town than it ever did' (Mass Observation 1943: 74). The ratio of on-licences to people fell from one for every 201 people in 1871 to one for every 458 in 1821 to one for every 761 persons by 1971. Between 1951 and 1971 the number of on-licences in England and Wales fell by 13 per cent from 73,421 to 64,087, of which 61,000 were pubs (Jennings 2007). Although there was a rise in the number of on-licenses granted in the 1980s and '90s, the British Beer and Pub Association (BBPA) estimates the number of pubs in the UK fell from around 66,000 in 1986 to 57,503 in 2007 (All-Party Parliamentary Beer Group [APPBG] 2008, BBPA 2009).

A recent Morgan Stanley analysis of the state of the leased pub trade (those pubs let out to tenants by pub companies or brewers) found that there were increased numbers of licensees leaving the industry, with the biggest pub landlords Enterprise Inns and Punch Taverns showing increased proportions of their estate available to lease: up from 12 and 14 per cent respectively to 14 per cent and 16 per cent over the course of 2008 (Rollo *et al* 2008).

The Morgan Stanley report further concluded that 'trading remains poor, the leased pub business model is coming under pressure, balance sheet risk is growing, and we think the (pub) companies need to focus on paying down debt' (Rollo 2008: 3). It has become apparent that the large pub companies that own so many of Britain's community pubs are under significant financial pressure, as are their licensees. The report concluded that licensees in 17 per cent of pubs owned by Enterprise Inns and 28 per cent of those owned by Punch Taverns were making a profit of under £20,000 a year. This is what they estimate to be a minimum level to make it worth running a pub, amounting to a profit of just £3.30 an hour each for a couple, excluding accommodation benefits, which is lower than the national minimum wage (ibid).

The licensee of an estate pub in Hackney, East London, vividly describes the situation in his local area, showing how many pubs are either closing or having to rapidly change their business in order to survive:

> 'On the Hackney Road, they're all strip joints. There's one pub left, the Jones' Arms. On Kingsland Road they're all gone…there's a gastro pub, the Fox, with candles, where people go to get something to eat. There's the Lock Tavern…they're living off the rooms. They make their money upstairs, not downstairs. The Wetherspoons is social security. There's the Dolphin, they live off the rooms and they're open all night. Over at The London Fields, they're on the verge of closing down. The Hare they do jazz on a Sunday night, the Dundee are an estate agents, the Salmon and Ball get passing trade because they're near the station, the Carpenters is a music pub. The Gun is still there, the Rising Sun, that's gone. We've been in a recession for five years.' **Licensee, Hackney, East London**

The geography of pub closures

ippr commissioned colleagues at Sheffield University to analyse CGA Strategy's pub closure figures by parliamentary constituency and by region of the country. Figure 2.1 shows the percentage change in the number of pubs per parliamentary constituency mapped out across the country. Table 2.1 shows the breakdown of pub closures by region.

This data on the geography of pub closures does not show any obvious pattern. Most parliamentary constituencies and all regions of the country show falls in the numbers of pubs since 2005. But it is clear that some regions have been hit more than others: the West Midlands, Scotland and the North West have seen very sharp falls in pub numbers in the last four years. It is less clear what the reason for this variation might be.

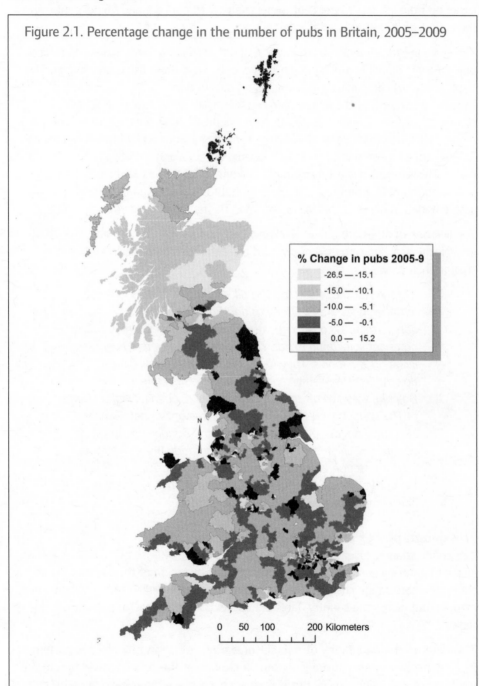

Figure 2.1. Percentage change in the number of pubs in Britain, 2005–2009

% Change in pubs 2005-9

-26.5 — -15.1
-15.0 — -10.1
-10.0 — -5.1
-5.0 — -0.1
0.0 — 15.2

0   50   100   200 Kilometers

Source: Data from CGA Strategy, mapped by John Pritchard, Sheffield University

Table 2.1. Regional breakdown of pub closures			
Region/country	No. of pubs 2005	Net pubs closed 2005–09	% pubs closed 2005–09
West Midlands	6,013	-576	-9.6
Scotland	5,971	-562	-9.4
North West	8,513	-612	-7.2
East Midlands	5,259	-356	-6.8
South East	8,521	-530	-6.2
Wales	4,147	-236	-5.7
East of England	5,562	-311	-5.6
Yorks and Humber	6,181	-322	-5.2
South West	6,507	-334	-5.1
London	6,583	-329	-5.0
North East	2,691	-103	-3.8

ippr asked colleagues at Sheffield University to explore some potential reasons for explaining why pub closure rates might be higher in some areas than others. They examined the correlation at constituency level between pub closures and two other variables: the level of deprivation and smoking rates. The latter was intended to allow us to explore the impact of the ban on smoking in public places.

Deprivation
Deprivation can be studied, in England only, by using the Indices of Multiple Deprivation 2007 – or IMD2007 (see Communities and Local Government 2007). IMD2007 is published at Lower Super Output Area level, which is a smaller geographical area than the parliamentary constituencies for which we have the pub closures data. Therefore, to enable comparison, the IMD2007 data was used to make estimates of the deprivation score at parliamentary constituency level. A correlation can then be calculated between the percentage of pubs that have closed in each area, and the IMD2007 score.

The correlation coefficient is 0.22. This shows that there is a weak positive association between the area level of deprivation and the number of pub closures.

Rates of smoking
The NHS Information Centre for health and social care, in its publication *Healthy Lifestyle Behaviours* (2008), estimated the percentage of people who smoke in each Middle Super Output Area of England. In a similar procedure to the IMD data, this data was used to make estimates of the percentage of people smoking at parliamentary constituency level.

The correlation coefficient is 0.14: a very weak positive association at this geographical level between rates of smoking and pub closures.

Conclusion

The analysis was tentative and intended to find a quick indication of the reason why some parts of the country have suffered more than others. The analysis shows that there are only weak positive correlations between pub closures per constituency and deprivation levels and smoking rates.

To take the geographical analysis further we would need to examine the link between pub closures and deprivation and/or smoking rates at smaller geographical levels, such as ward level. If there are links they may be more apparent at that level. The figures also only show net changes which do not tell the whole story of which pubs are closing and where. Finally, for a full analysis we would need to explore the impact of a range of other factors that might explain the variations across the country.

Explaining rising pub closures

Returning to the nationwide picture, what is causing so many pubs to close? Below we examine a number of factors that are having varying effects.

The economic downturn

The health of the pub trade has always depended on the health of the wider economy. One of the earliest studies of pub-going behaviour in Britain found that reduced purchasing power was an important factor in the fall in the quantity of beer drunk between the late 19th century and the 1930s (Mass Observation 1943).

Figure 2.2 supports the notion that there is a causal link between alcohol consumption and economic growth, showing falls in UK alcohol consumption that correspond with the economic recessions of the early 1980s and 1990s. It then shows steady growth in consumption as the economy grew substantially during the last decade and a half.

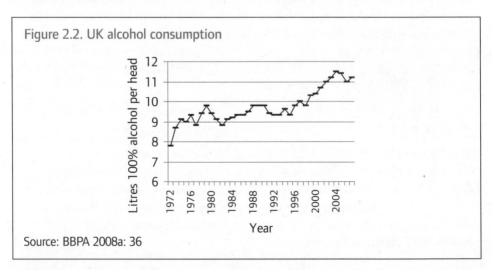

Figure 2.2. UK alcohol consumption

Source: BBPA 2008a: 36

In line with this trend, the recent credit crunch and subsequent recession have hit the pub trade once more, with the coming year expected to be particularly tough.

Changes to communities

It is not simply the current recession that has been putting pressure on licensees. As we have seen, despite rising alcohol consumption overall, pub numbers have been falling for well over a decade. In part this is because many of the old residential communities on which community pubs used to depend have changed, some out of all recognition. For example, over the last 50 years many rural villages have moved from being communities with local employment to dormitory villages or second home locations. The community around the village pub has changed and residents with more widely dispersed friendship networks no longer 'nip down the local'.

Another example is the former industrial areas where pubs served a male working class population on its way home from work. As those old industries have gone, so too have those large drinking populations.

Finally, many of our towns and cities now have much more transient populations: in London for example 15 per cent of the population have lived in their present location for less than a year (Travers et al 2007). These more mobile urban populations are less likely to gain an attachment to a local pub.

Changes to tastes and lifestyles

One of the major factors behind this longer-term decline is changing consumer tastes in alcoholic beverages. Beer is the mainstay of pub incomes and yet beer consumption has fallen significantly in the last thirty years (see Figure 2.3). We have gone from an overwhelmingly beer-drinking country to a nation with more continental tastes, in particular a growing love for wine.

The pub has also faced competition from alternative leisure pursuits. The relative affluence of the last decade saw a significant rise in the number of people eating out

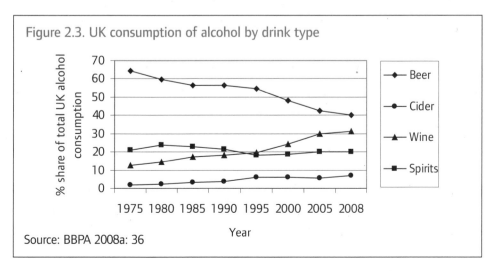

Figure 2.3. UK consumption of alcohol by drink type

Source: BBPA 2008a: 36

in restaurants and there was a threefold increase in the rate of new restaurant openings between 1992 and 2007 (BBC News online 2007). The rise of the 'gastro-pub' has been one way in which pub owners have responded to this trend. There has also been a significant rise in cinema attendances in recent years, which reached a 38-year high in the summer of 2007 (*The Independent* 2007).

Even more significant for the pub trade has been the shift towards drinking at home. The share of alcohol being purchased in shops and supermarkets has increased dramatically at the expense of pubs and bars. Figure 2.4 shows that the proportion of beer being sold in pubs and bars fell from over 90 per cent in 1975 to just 56 per cent in 2007.

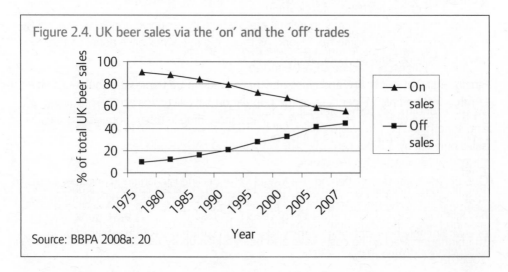

Figure 2.4. UK beer sales via the 'on' and the 'off' trades

Source: BBPA 2008a: 20

In part this reflects a wider shift towards staying at home due to the growth of forms of home entertainment such as television, DVD players and video games. In recent years, however, there has been a further significant factor encouraging people to drink at home – price.

Prices

In recent decades beer prices have been rising well above the rate of inflation and much of this has been due to increases in beer duty, which in the last decade alone rose from 25p a pint, in 1998, to 36p a pint, in 2008 (BBPA 2008a). These tax pressures are only set to intensify in the years ahead: the 2008 budget introduced an increase in beer duty of 6 per cent above inflation and an annual 2 per cent above inflation escalator up to 2013 (BBPA 2008b).

The main problem for the pub trade is that supermarkets and off licences have been able to sell their beer much more cheaply than pubs and bars. Since 1987 there has been a 161 percentage point increase in the retail price of 'on-trade' beer, compared with just a 46 percentage point increase in the price of off-trade beer (BBPA 2008a).

Today, beer in the on-trade retails at £4.16 per litre, compared with £1.75 a litre in the off-trade (Ernst and Young 2007).

In more recent years competition has become increasingly aggressive, with some supermarkets able to sell alcohol at or below cost, using them as 'loss leaders' to attract customers through their doors to spend their money on other goods. Many licensees blame these discounts for the decline in the pub trade:

> 'The trade is dying a death. You can't compete with the supermarkets. I was in Tesco before Christmas and they were selling 400ml cans of John Smiths at 15 cans for £7, 40 cans for under £20 – that's 45p a can. You can't compete with that.'
> **Former licensee, Macclesfield**

> 'You can get beer for 50p a can at Tesco. This is a takeaway society. People tank up before they come out.'
> **Licensee, Hackney, East London**

As the economy has turned sour, it is the pubs that are suffering more than the shops and supermarkets: whereas on-sales fell by 10.6 per cent in April to June 2008, off-sales only fell by 3.8 per cent over the same period (APPBG 2008).

Costs
Pub licensees have also faced rising costs. Increased materials and utilities prices have been passed on by the brewers in the higher wholesale price of beer. A shortage of malting barley and rising demand for bio-fuels have seen barley prices increase faster than inflation. Packaging costs have also been driven up by rising energy prices (BBPA 2008b).

Licensees have seen their own operating costs increase. For example, licensees have had to spend increasing amounts on entertainment to stay competitive. A recent survey by the Association of Licensed Multiple Retailers (ALMR) found that their members' third largest cost was entertainment. The 2003 Licensing Act abolished the 'two in a bar' rule, which had meant that no licence was required for putting on two live performers. In addition many pubs rely on live football to bring people through the door and Sky television fees have continued to increase. These are calculated on the rateable value of the pub and this can be disproportionately expensive for small pubs in higher rated rural areas (APPBG 2008).

The impact of the ban on smoking in public places on the trade is the subject of intense debate. The ban is overwhelmingly popular with the general public: one year on from its introduction 76 per cent of the public supported it (Deparment of Health 2008). However, its introduction did place a cost burden on pubs which should be recognised: the ALMR found that the ban had cost their members on average £6000, largely due to spending money on new outdoor smoking areas.

The impact of the smoking ban on the numbers visiting pubs varies across the trade. A survey for the *Publican* trade paper found that 73 per cent of licensees supported the ban staying in place and a quarter of pubs said they had even attracted new customers because of the ban (Sky News online 2007). On the other hand 'landlocked' pubs without access to outdoor space are reported to have suffered a significant loss in trade, particularly during the winter months when people are reluctant to go outside for a cigarette (*The Observer* 2008, Mintel 2008).

Our brief analysis of why pub closure rates differ between parliamentary constituencies indicates that there is a weak positive correlation between closure rates and smoking rates in England. However, this may be hiding other explanatory variables: for example it may simply be because smoking rates are higher in more deprived communities. This is a topic that requires further research.

The introduction of a new licensing regime with the 2003 Licensing Act also imposed a significant one-off cost for pubs, given that all licensees had to apply for new premises licences. Under the new regime applying for even minor variations to premises costs significantly more than under the previous system (APPBG 2008).

Government regulation is rightly concerned with promoting public health and reducing crime. However, it is worth pointing out that the regulatory framework currently takes no account of the differential ability of operators to cope with the increased cumulative costs. These costs are easily swallowed by the large pub chains who, incidentally, also tend to run the town centre bars that are most often associated with excessive drinking. Most community pub licensees, by contrast, are sole operators having to work within extremely tight margins, for whom the cumulative cost of increased regulation is much more difficult to carry.

This is not an argument for repealing these specific examples of regulation: the Licensing Act provides a much more rational framework for managing licensed premises than that which existed before and the smoking ban is overwhelmingly popular with the general public. It is an argument, however, for providing some compensatory support for community pubs through other means.

The pubcos
One of the most fiercely contested issues in the pub trade is the behaviour of the large pub companies or 'pubcos'. Very many licensees argue that these companies are putting otherwise successful pubs out of business through excessively high rents and beer prices. As pubs have struggled in recent years, this issue has risen to the top of the industry agenda and has been the subject of two Parliamentary Select Committee inquiries. The second of these by the Business and Enterprise Committee will report later in 2009.

The two main allegations against the pubcos are that they are charging their tenants too much for their beer and that their rents are too high and calculated in a non-transparent way.

On the first point, pubco tenants usually have to buy all their beer and most of their other drinks (in some cases all their drink) from their pubco's price list – this relationship is known as the 'beer tie' or 'wet rent'. The beer tie of course used to exist under the old integrated model (removed by the beer orders) under which tenants of a brewery pub had to exclusively sell that brewer's beer. Pubco tenants argue that they are being charged much more for their beer than if they bought it on the free market and that the pubcos have been increasing their prices well above inflation in recent years.

In the course of our research we were told by licensees:

> *'We were hammered by the pubco. The rent was about £40,000 a year, add on £1000 a month in rates, and national insurance contributions. As for the beer, you end up paying top dollar for that – £50 to £60 more than you could get it from the wholesaler.'* **Former licensee, Macclesfield**

> *'The pub companies are middle men like the Sicilian mafia. They charge above market rent and you have to buy everything off them.'* **Licensee, estate pub, Hackney**

> *'I run tied and free-of-tie pubs. I can get Carling free of tie for £63 for an 11 gallon keg. Enterprise sells the same keg at £112. That's about 60p a pint difference.'* **Licensee, South London**

> *'The pub companies get people in on a false promise. As a free house we have an advantage. Everywhere else you pay £2.45 for a pint – you come in here and its £2.'* **Licensee, free house pub, County Durham**

> *'I'm lucky. I have a guest beer provision in my lease, which means that I can sell a guest ale much cheaper than the beer I buy from the pubco list. That beer outsells the others four to one.'* **Licensee, Central London**

The price quoted by the pubcos is not actually different from the wholesale price of the beer. Rather, the difference comes about because pubcos negotiate discounts from the breweries, the bulk of which are then not passed on by the pubcos to their tenants. In 2004 the Trade and Industry Select Committee concluded that this meant that on average tied tenants were paying £50 a barrel more than they would pay if they were a freehouse operator.

Pubco tenants also have to share any revenue made from 'amusement with prizes' (AWP) machines in their pub. The Trade and Industry Select Committee found that even though machines installed through the pubco had a higher turnover than those operating in freehouses, because the pubco generally took 50 per cent of the revenue, pubco lessees were earning considerably less than freehouse operators from such machines. The committee argued that the pubcos could not plausibly claim to contribute significantly to the success of the machines, justifying taking half of the profits on them. Adding the machine tie to the beer tie, the Select Committee estimated that in 2004 there was an extra £70 a barrel cost involved in being a tenant of a pubco compared with being a free of tie operator (Trade and Industry Select Committee 2004).

The second claim against the pubcos is that the way their rents are calculated lacks transparency and consequently many tenants feel they are paying too much. For new leases pubcos calculate the rent on the basis of a projection of the fair maintainable level of trade (FMT) a competent hypothetical untied tenant would be expected to achieve. This projects 'wet' sales, food sales, room rentals and takings from AWP machines. It subtracts estimated costs from the FMT and the rent valuation is based on a percentage of the remaining profit, known as the 'divisible balance'. The Select Committee found that typically 50 per cent of this would then go to the pubco.

Many tenants have complained about a lack of transparency in how a fair maintainable level of trade is calculated and pubcos generally provide only very basic information to potential tenants such as expected levels of sales and costs. This takes no account of the actual previous pattern of trade and there have been complaints that costs have been considerably under-estimated, reducing tenants' margins.

There have also been concerns about 'upward only rent review' clauses being written into leases, which take no account of falling actual levels of trade. Some successful operators have argued more widely that a profit-based system of rent penalises success, simply because the better someone's business performs, the higher the rent claimed by the pubco.

> 'There are several pubs round here that have closed – owned by Punch Taverns and Enterprise and Greene King. The three horrors of the industry. They have been closing down businesses like wild fire. Once they become a successful pub they put the rent up and kill the business.' **Licensee, freehouse, village pub, Essex**

Finally, there are concerns about the lack of an accessible and independent arbitration system, which leaves many tenants faced with a choice between accepting what is on offer or taking on an expensive legal challenge (HoC Trade and Industry Select Committee 2004).

Against these claims the pubcos argue that they provide a low-cost way of entering the trade: people would otherwise need funds to buy their own pub, but with just £20-30,000 they can set up a small business. They also argue that tenants benefit from a range of 'special commercial or financial advantages', including training, legal advice, support from Business Development Managers and ongoing investment to enhance the business.

Others point out that the buying power of the large pubcos prevents the brewers from putting prices up even further and that ending the tie might simply benefit the brewers and disadvantage smaller barrelage operators in particular, who would be unable to secure large discounts. Tony Payne, Chief Executive of the Federation of Licensed Victuallers Associations, told ippr that 'small barrelage pubs would not do well out of it'.

In light of all of this the 2004 Select Committee concluded that 'the immediately quantifiable cost of the tie is usually balanced by benefits available to tenants' (HoC Trade and Industry Select Committee 2004: 54). However, since then it has become clear that the tie has remained unpopular with licensees: a 2008 survey of 1000 licensees by the Federation of Small Businesses found that 94 per cent wanted the beer tie to be removed and 99 per cent reported that little had changed since the 2004 enquiry (*The Publican* 2008).

The situation is thought by analysts to have deteriorated because of the precarious financial status of the large pubcos, which borrowed heavily against their assets in the days of booming property prices now at an end. Punch Taverns needs to finance a net debt of £4.5 billion and in the 20 weeks to 10 January 2009 its profits fell by 12 per cent (*Financial Times* 2009a). Enterprise Inns has a net debt of £3.7 billion and in the 16 weeks to 17 January 2009 its profits fell by 8 per cent (*Financial Times* 2009c). Both of these big pubcos have seen their share price plummet by over 90 per cent in the last year, among the worst hit by the recent share price falls outside the collapsed banks. According to Mark Brumby, leisure analyst at Blue Oar: 'They've been over-geared for a number of years and as the concern attached to that has grown, they've been hit' (*The Independent* 2009).

This is thought by analysts to have added to the financial pressure on the tenants. A 2008 Morgan Stanley report found that a significant number of pubco tied pubs were over-rented in relation to their underlying profitability: 17 per cent of Enterprise pubs and 28 per cent of Punch pubs were 'uneconomic' given the very low level of profits they were making. The report added that 'pubco profits have risen somewhat faster than lessee profits over the last five years, so we would not be surprised if this has squeezed the lower end of the market' (Rollo *et al* 2008: 5). Between 2003 and 2007 for example, profits at Enterprise Inns increased by 36 per cent, compared with just 27 per cent for the lessees, when one would expect profits to increase faster for the operator (ibid).

Unfortunately there are gaps in the evidence base on the impact of the beer tie, as operated by the big pubcos. To gain a full picture of the impact of the tied model we would need data that directly compared the failure rates of tied and non-tied pubs: on the basis of the tenants' case we would expect tied pubs to be performing much worse than free-of-tie houses. The BBPA informed the Business and Enterprise Committee that pub closures are actually higher among freehouse operators (Business and Enterprise Committee 2009). However, this data does not tell us whether pubco tenants are at a greater disadvantage because of the tie, simply because it does not take into account the numbers of tenants whose businesses fail and who are then replaced by another tenant. The pubcos do not publish these figures showing the level of churn on their estates, which means we cannot directly compare the success of tied and non-tied pubs.

However recent trading patterns show that, as the recession bites, tied pubs are being out-performed by the managed chains like Wetherspoons. This is likely to be because the managed chains have the freedom to cut prices and offer significant discounts to their customers, as many have been doing in response to the downturn in the economy:

- Mitchell & Butlers saw its sales increase in the latter half of 2008 on the back of discounted food and drink. It claims to be offering 40p a pint less for a standard lager than the same drink in a leased pub (*Morning Advertiser* 2009, *Financial Times* 2009e).
- Greene King's directly managed pubs have been outperforming its leased estate (*Financial Times* 2009d).
- JD Wetherspoons reported increased sales in the last quarter of 2008 on the back of its 99p-a-pint promotion (*Financial Times* 2009b).
- Fullers also reported increased sales in their managed houses, compared with falling sales in their leased houses (*Financial Times* 2009e).

So while the evidence base is incomplete, there is considerable evidence that licensees in the tied leased sector are facing significant additional pressure, because of the higher price they are paying for their beer. Any strategy to reverse pub closures therefore needs to include reform to this business model as currently operated by the large pubcos.

Summary

Our research has found that Britain's pubs are in trouble. The number of pubs closing has been rising and is now at its highest level for years. This is not simply due to the impact of the credit crunch and the current economic climate – the number of pubs across the country has been falling for decades. In part this is because of changing consumer tastes and lifestyles: there are alternative places to drink and beer is less popular. This means pubs have to change what it is they are offering in order to survive. Pubs are also under pressure from increased alcohol duties, higher operational costs and cut-price supermarket competition. There are real concerns about how the tied lease model is affecting pubco tenants. In the next chapter we address why all of this matters.

3. Why pubs matter

'There is nothing which has yet been contrived by man, by which so much happiness is produced as by a good tavern or inn.' **Samuel Johnson, 1791** (Kingsnorth 2008: 21)

'To write of the English inn is to write of England itself…as familiar in the national consciousness as the oak and the ash and the village green and the church spire.' **Thomas Burke, 1930** (*The English Inn,* Herbert Jenkins 1947: 7)

'The one human corner, a centre not for beer but bonhomie; the one place where after dark the collective heart of the nation could be seen and felt, beating resolute and strong.'
A.P. Herbert MP on the role of the pub during the Second World War (Jennings 2007: 209)

The public house is more than just a retail business: it plays an important role at the heart of many local communities, providing a hub through which social networks can be maintained and extended. We have already shown that the pub trade is in trouble and set out a number of reasons for this. In this chapter we turn to the impact of these pub closures on local communities by assessing why pubs matter and explaining why public policy has a legitimate role in promoting and supporting them.

Social networks

One of the most important contributions pubs make to local community life is that they act as hubs for the development of social networks between local people. Our national opinion poll found that outside the home the pub scored the highest of any location as a place where people 'meet and get together with others in their neighbourhood': 36 per cent of respondents said that pubs were important for this purpose, compared with 32 per cent saying other people's houses, 20 per cent saying local cafes and restaurants and 15 per cent saying local shops (see Figure 3.1).

Of course this was not true evenly across all groups: among men the pub scored higher than their own home as a site of social interaction, whereas among women the pub came third in importance, behind one's own home and other people's homes. However, the pub was marginally more important for women as a site of social interaction than local cafes and restaurants or local shops (Figure 3.2). The pub is more significant as a local hub for younger people as opposed to older people (Figure 3.3). However, the pub scored the highest of all places outside one's own home for all social classes bar one ('C1') and across all groups the pub scored higher than any institution except the home or other people's homes (Figure 3.4).

The following graphs, Figures 3.1-3.4 (source: CAMRA Tracking Omnibus Survey January 2009), show responses to the question:

> *'Which three of the following places on this list would you say are most important to you personally to meet and get together with others in your neighbourhood?'*

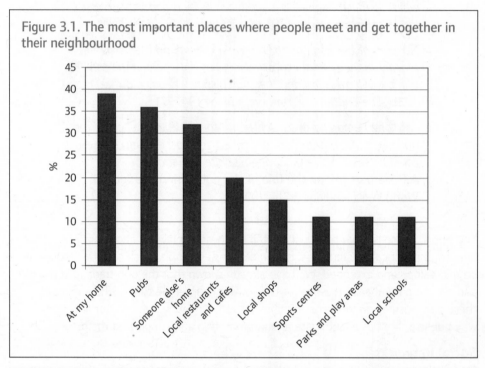

Figure 3.1. The most important places where people meet and get together in their neighbourhood

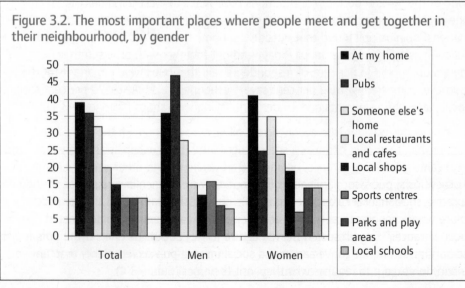

Figure 3.2. The most important places where people meet and get together in their neighbourhood, by gender

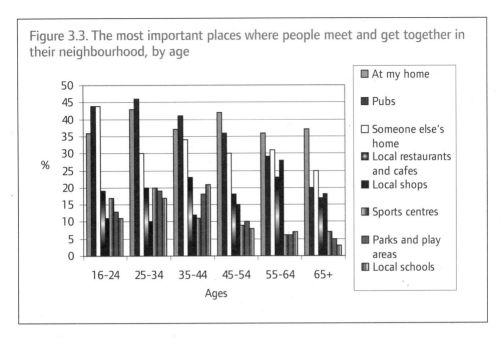

Figure 3.3. The most important places where people meet and get together in their neighbourhood, by age

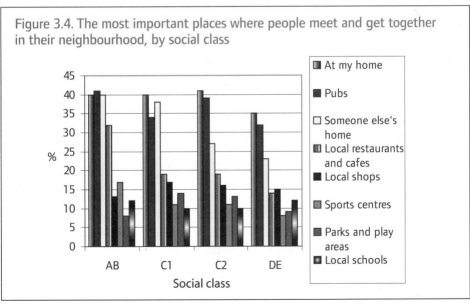

Figure 3.4. The most important places where people meet and get together in their neighbourhood, by social class

Local pubs support social networks in two main ways: they allow people to strengthen existing social networks by meeting up with friends and family and they provide a place where people are able to meet new people and extend their networks of acquaintances (Social Issues Research Centre [SIRC] 2008). This role of the pub as an important setting for conversation and social interaction was repeatedly emphasised when we asked pub regulars why they visit their local pub.

> *'It's not only the beer, it's the conversational company and you'll find that good pubs attract good people.'* **Man, village pub, Cambridgeshire**

> *'[I come here] to meet him and her, those two rogues there, and Bob and Mike and Candy…and Bill and Frank. If you want to know why I come to a pub – one word – people.'* **Man, rural pub, Hertfordshire**

> *'It's somewhere to have a conversation.'* **Woman, rural pub, Hertfordshire**

> *'It's more like the old days, the '70s and '80s. Proper conversations. You don't see any people in here with a bloody laptop do you? It has got wi-fi – but people talk.'* **Man, inner-city pub, Hackney**

> *'The essence of this pub is conversation…you'll generally find someone in here that you know and you'll generally find a few strangers in here that you can have a conversation with anyway.'* **Man, inner-city pub, Hackney**

Contrary to the old image of pubs as anti-family places, research shows that of those people who visit a pub more than once a month, over 50 per cent of women and over 40 per cent of men go to the pub with their partner – and importantly 35 per cent go with other members of their family, which is especially the case for those aged 45 and over. Researchers concluded that: 'the pub may be one of the few remaining social institutions that actively preserves the extended family and inter-generational relationships' (SIRC 2008: 26-27).

While the majority of pub-goers say they visit the pub with existing close friends, 28 per cent of male pub-goers and 21 per cent of female pub-goers say they find it easy to meet new people in the pub (ibid). This ease with which people can make new acquaintances in a pub environment has been found by anthropologists to be due to the low cost of entering 'pub conversation'. Pub etiquette means that you can start a conversation with someone in the knowledge that there is no obligation to talk longer than you want. In pubs, particularly at the bar and even in the toilets, people drift in and out of conversations with complete strangers in a way they rarely do in other contexts, on public transport or at the supermarket check-out, for example (ibid). One author claims, not unreasonably, that 'the bar counter in a pub is possibly the only site in the British Isles in which friendly conversation with strangers is considered entirely appropriate and normal behaviour' (Fox 1996: 5).

One important consequence of the pub's role as a place where one's social networks are maintained and extended is that a startling 27 per cent of British couples say they met their current partner in a pub (ibid).

Of course, we should note that not everybody goes to the pub to socialise and indeed another important characteristic of pub culture is if people wish to keep themselves to themselves, this is generally respected by other pub-goers. The pub can bring friends and family together but it also provides a place where people can escape from their work or family lives.

> *'There are some regulars in here who don't actually talk to you that much, but that's their prerogative. Not everyone likes to socialise, they want to be on their own...you can do what you like.'* **Man, inner city pub, Hackney**

> *'There are some people who come in here and treat it as a second lounge, because they don't want to be at home on their own or because they live with other people and they don't want to be in their pockets all the time – it's a second lounge, where they can talk to other people, but if they want to sit there quietly they can.'* **Landlady, rural pub, Hertfordshire**

> *'I come in here because it's NOT a meeting place – I come here to avoid my neighbours, I don't want to meet them.'* **Man, rural pub, Hertfordshire**

Given that the pub is the most important place outside the home for people to meet their neighbours, the impact of pub closures on the quality of existing social networks can be severe. One community campaigner against a pub closure in his Cambridgeshire village describes the impact on community life:

> *'It closed for a year. The community is 20 per cent people who are very private, 20 per cent people who are in and out of each other's places often because they have kids – and then there's 60 per cent in the middle. It was that 60 per cent that died. Every community needs somewhere to bounce off itself. People meet in the pub, finds things in common, borrow things. Village halls can't do that – you can't just drop in and relax.'* **Community pub campaigner, Cambridgeshire village**

The role of pubs as meeting points is of course especially important in villages where there is no other social centre for people to meet and interact:

> *'The pub is an integral part of the village – there's only us and the shop. We rely heavily on a good band of regulars, it acts as a meeting place. If the pub wasn't here there'd be nowhere for people to meet. There's a community centre, but no one really uses that.'* **Landlady, village pub, Lancashire**

This is why there have been so many campaigns to prevent village pub closures. In some cases it has become apparent that breweries or pub companies would prefer to knock a pub down and build housing on lucrative rural sites. In many cases local residents have successfully petitioned local authorities to prevent a change of planning use from commercial to residential use, arguing that their local pub remains viable and believing it to be an important local amenity. In other cases local residents have felt so strongly they have actually clubbed together to buy their local pub.

Economic impact

In addition to these community benefits community pubs add a great deal to local economies – and beer bought through pubs adds more value to local economies than beer bought through supermarkets.

Nationally, the pub industry amounts to 2 per cent of national GDP and community pubs provide 350,000 full- or part-time jobs (APPBG 2008). In all, the brewing and pub sector generates £28 billion of economic activity, compared with £20 billion by the airline sector, £18 billion by the radio and TV sector and £18 billion by clothes retailing (BBPA 2008b).

Four out of five jobs created through the sale and production of beer are in the hospitality sector (pubs, bars, clubs and restaurants) (Ernst and Young 2007). The UK accounts for 19 per cent of all hospitality jobs linked to brewing in Europe, with only Germany creating more such jobs. This is largely because more beer is bought in pubs in the UK than in other countries and pubs generate more jobs per litre of beer sold than shops and supermarkets do. In terms of employment generation, it makes more sense to encourage the sale of beer through pubs than through shops and supermarkets. As we know, the policy framework currently encourages exactly the opposite.

At the local level, it is estimated that each pub injects an average of £80,000 into their local economy. Pubs also support small and regional breweries much more than shops and supermarkets do: these breweries sell 76 per cent of their beer through pubs. In turn these regional brewers add more value to the national and local economy per litre than the big national brewers, who are less likely to source goods and services locally. The regional brewers are also more labour intensive and generate more jobs: 8 per 10,000 hectolitres of beer produced, compared to 3.5 for the national brewers (Ernst and Young 2007).

Pubs make a disproportionately large contribution to the public purse: every pint sold in a pub raises twice as much tax as that sold through the off-trade (BBPA 2008b). The total level of tax raised from the sale of alcoholic drinks was £14.7 billion in 2007/08, which is a significant 3.7 per cent of total government revenue. Added to this is the £175 million raised through duty and VAT from fruit machines (APPBG 2008).

Crime and disorder

Pubs are not always associated with making a positive contribution to the community and we know that alcohol consumption is a significant factor in driving levels of violent crime and disorder. According to the 2007/08 British Crime Survey, victims believed the offender(s) to be under the influence of alcohol in 45 per cent of all violent incidents, similar to the level in the 2006/07 Survey (46 per cent) (Home Office 2009).[1]

Before addressing the role of community pubs in this we should make two important qualifications. First, let us put recent concerns about alcohol-related crime into some historical context. Any read through pub history will show that cyclical moral panics about how much people are drinking (especially young people, working people and women) are a constant theme. For example, the 'gin craze' of the eighteenth century was thought to have led to an increase in drunkenness that disturbed the upper classes and far surpassed anything that has happened in recent years. By 1751 'one in four houses in London was a dram shop and virtually the entire population was semi-permanently drunk' (Haydon 1994: 55).

Following the Duke of Wellington's decision to liberalise the licensing regime and abolish beer duties in 1830, commentators and politicians perceived there to be a rise in drunkenness and proclaimed the nation to be teetering on the brink of chaos:

> *'The new beer bill has begun its operation. Everybody is drunk. Those who are not singing are sprawling. The sovereign people are in a beastly state.'* **Sydney Smith** (quoted in Haydon 1994: 187-188)

> *'The words "licensed to be drunk on the premises" are by the people interpreted as applicable to the customers as well as the liquor.'* **Lord Palmerston** (quoted in Haydon 1994: 188)

Moving into the twentieth century, consider how familiar the following description of closing time on a weekend in Blackpool in the 1930s would sound to newspaper readers of the present day:

> *'At closing time back and front streets crowded, some people dancing, men and women doing foxtrots and a group of women trying to do a fling. Three observers independently claim that at least 25 per cent of the crowd are drunk...(later) Along the promenade the air is full of beersmell, that overcomes seasmell. It arises from people breathing. A swirling moving mass of*

---

1. We refer to British Crime Survey data here because we know that police records that say which crimes are alcohol-related are problematic, simply because different forces record the data differently. For instance, one survey found that almost 30 per cent of local police forces kept no records at all of the extent to which crimes are alcohol related (SIRC 2002).

mostly drunk people, singing, playing mouth organs, groups dancing about. Chaps fall over and their friends pick them up cheerfully and unconcernedly. At one spot a young man falls flat on his face, his friend picks him up and puts him over his shoulder, and lurches away with him. Immediately a fight starts among four young men: the crowd simply opens up to give them elbow room as it flows by; some stop to look on. One of the fighters is knocked out cold and the others carry him to the back of a stall and dump him there. Back streets are not so densely crowded, but even more drunks. In a litter of broken glass and bottles a woman sits by herself being noisily sick.'
Mass Observation (1943: 248)

So drunkenness is nothing new and there have been times in our history when it has been much worse than it is today.

Second, the link between aggression and alcohol consumption is not as straightforward as it is typically portrayed in the press. There is, of course, a biological impact from the chemical effects of consuming alcohol: alcohol interferes with primary cognitive ability by reducing a drinker's perceptual field. It also impairs the drinker's ability to communicate and opens the way to misunderstandings and misinterpretations (Marsh and Fox Kibby 1992). But cognitive impairment alone does not lead to violence. Most people who drink alcohol do not become aggressive and are perfectly capable of combining a few drinks with civilised behaviour. Indeed, in many other cultures drinking is more often associated with friendliness and gregariousness than aggression (ibid). There are therefore cultural and situational factors that must be accounted for in explaining why some people in some contexts become violent and aggressive when drinking (ibid, MCM Research 1990).

Nevertheless, even with these qualifications, it is clear from the BCS data that alcohol is a key driver behind violent crime in the UK, and not just street crime, but domestic violence as well. The question that concerns us here is how much of this crime can be attributed to community pubs.

Clearly problems occur in pubs as a result of alcohol consumption. And yet one study found that the majority of pubs experience less than one or two fights per year. Those experiencing regular trouble (a fight at least once a week) represented just 8 per cent of all pubs surveyed. 75 per cent of these incidents involved the pub manager, largely because they have to control behaviour and enforce the rules within the pub, such as by refusing to serve someone or asking them to leave (MCM Research 1990).

In our opinion poll, we asked people to specify which of a number of activities they had been involved in or observed in their local pub in the last six months (see Figure 3.5): 65 per cent of people said they had spent time with friends and family, 23 per cent said they had made new friends, 19 per cent had mixed with people they would not normally mix with and only 6 per cent said a crime or some form of anti-social behaviour had taken place. It is clear that violence takes place rarely and in a small minority of pubs.

Importantly, poor management style has been found to account for 40 per cent of the difference between pubs in terms of the level of violence. The next most significant factor in explaining why fights occur in some pubs and not others is the length of time the manager had been in place: well-trained managers who are in place for longer can significantly reduce the amount of trouble found in pubs (MCM Research 1990). It is also important to note that no such informal social control exists outside of the pub setting – in other words whereas responsible drinking can be incentivised, encouraged and ultimately enforced in a pub, there is no such control with alcohol bought in the supermarket and consumed at home or on the street.

It is also clear that the community pubs that are the focus of this research are generally not those experiencing problems of excessive drinking and related violence and disorder. Although there are no national figures to show the proportion of crime taking place in different parts of towns and cities, local data and police evidence show that the vast bulk of alcohol-related disorder takes place in town and city centres on a Friday and Saturday night (Marsh and Fox Kibby 1992).

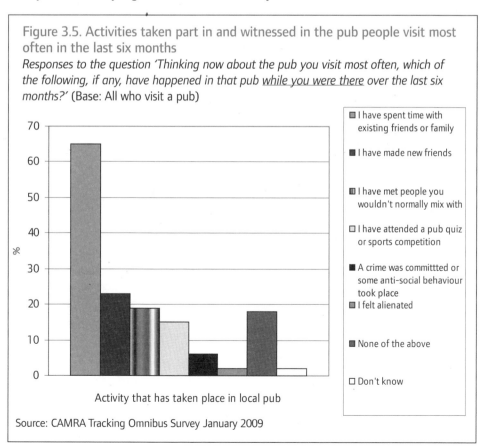

Figure 3.5. Activities taken part in and witnessed in the pub people visit most often in the last six months
Responses to the question 'Thinking now about the pub you visit most often, which of the following, if any, have happened in that pub while you were there over the last six months?' (Base: All who visit a pub)

Source: CAMRA Tracking Omnibus Survey January 2009

Community cohesion

'Community cohesion' has become a key public policy buzzword. Essentially, this refers to the effort to promote good relations between people from different walks of life. Our opinion poll found that pubs are perceived to be the most important social institution for promoting interactions between people from different backgrounds at the local level (see Figure 3.6). When asked where in the last six months they had mixed socially with people from a different background to their own, the pub was the most chosen location with 36 per cent, followed by the home at 26 per cent, work and college at 26 per cent and the local shops at 22 per cent.

This was true of people of all social classes and in so far as we can interpret this as referring to class among other identities, this supports the longstanding view that the pub is a great social leveller (SIRC 2008, Fox 1996). Indeed, our interviewees stressed the importance of the egalitarian character of pubs:

> *'You can be a prince or a pauper when you come in here and they talk to you at the same level.'* **Man, village pub, Cambridgeshire**

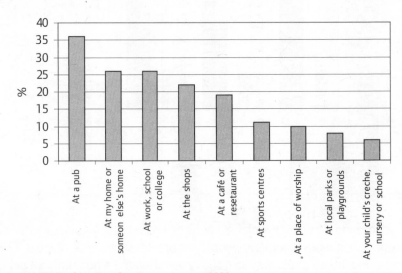

Figure 3.6. Places where people mix socially with people from a different background

In response to the question: Which three of the following places on this list would you say are most important to you personally to meet and get together with others in your neighbourhood?

Source: CAMRA Tracking Omnibus Survey January 2009

> '*It wouldn't matter if you had tuppence or two thousand pounds – you'd be treated the same, at that level bar.*' **Man, village pub, Cambridgeshire**

> '*You get a great cross-section of people in here – from girls in jodhpurs to men in suits. That's a how a pub should be – it's classless.*' **Landlord, rural pub, Hertfordshire**

Of course, the pub-going population is not representative of society as a whole. Historically, pubs have been heavily dominated by males and to some extent remain so: even though female attendance in pubs is much higher than in the past, men still make up the bulk of the 'regular' pub crowd: according to our research, whereas 34 per cent of men overall attend a pub once a week or more, just 12 per cent of women do (Figure 3.7). Very few women say they would be happy going to a pub on their own, which contrasts markedly with men's attitudes (SIRC 2008).

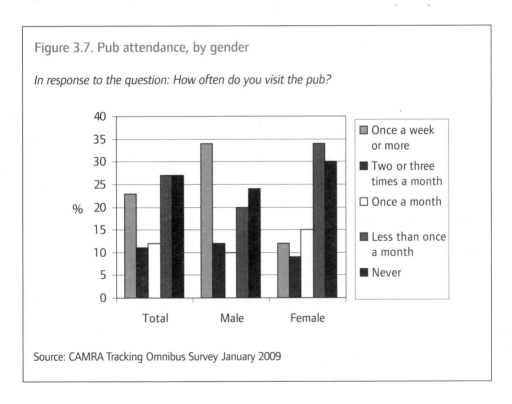

Figure 3.7. Pub attendance, by gender

In response to the question: How often do you visit the pub?

Source: CAMRA Tracking Omnibus Survey January 2009

As well as showing a gender imbalance, pubs tend to attract younger and middle-aged people much more than older people: Figure 3.8 shows that whereas 73 per cent of respondents to our survey said they ever attended a pub, only 57 per cent of the over-65s did.

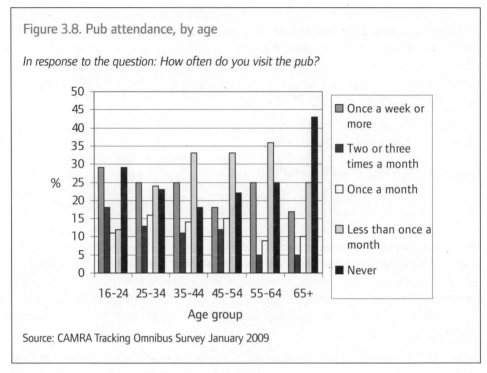

Figure 3.8. Pub attendance, by age

In response to the question: How often do you visit the pub?

Source: CAMRA Tracking Omnibus Survey January 2009

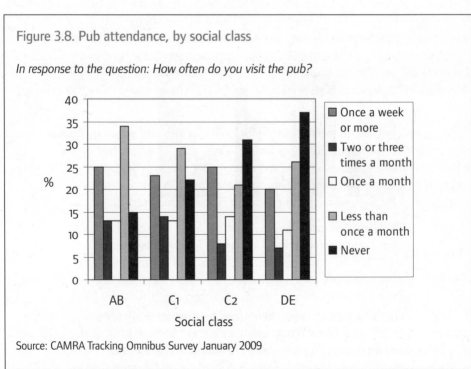

Figure 3.8. Pub attendance, by social class

In response to the question: How often do you visit the pub?

Source: CAMRA Tracking Omnibus Survey January 2009

In contrast to the image of the pub as a working-class institution, in so far as there is a social class bias to pub attendance it is today the other way around: whereas 85 per cent of professionals said they ever attended a pub, the level falls to 63 per cent among the lowest earning 'DE' occupational class (Figure 3.9). The figures are not broken down by religion, but of course one can expect that pub-going is virtually non-existent among some faith communities.

So, pubs are an important local institution for social mixing, but some groups still go to pubs more frequently than do others.

Community and civic participation

Pubs are, of course, primarily places for relaxation and leisure. Most of the organised activities in pubs tend to be oriented towards entertainment such as pub quizzes, darts competitions, pool leagues.

Pubs have also long been associated with politics: in the eighteenth century, working men's clubs, unions and Jacobite clubs made pubs their meeting places. The radical London Corresponding Society first met in the Bell, Exeter Street in 1791, beginning a long-standing association between the labour movement and the public house. At around the same time the Tory October Club used to meet in the Bell on King Street and rival Tory and Whig ale houses were set up in opposition to each other.

Pubs also host community oriented events and activities that add considerably to local civic life, and have done so for many decades. Mass Observation noted in its path-breaking study of pub life in Bolton in the 1930s that 'amongst pub-goers, groups exist whose activities though they are not directly connected with drinking play a considerable role in the life of pubs'. These included secret societies (such as the curiously named Ancient Noble Order of United Oddfellows and the Royal and Antediluvian Order of Buffaloes), savings clubs and trade unions (Mass Observation 1943).

Today, pubs continue to provide rooms for local charities and voluntary groups to hold their meetings in and particularly in local villages, pubs often provide the only community meeting space, outside the church. One landlady set out for us the wide range of civic and community activity that takes place in her pub, ranging from discussion of local issues to the organisation of charitable events:

> *'They'll discuss local issues…there's a lot of discussion recently about the widening of the M25 which is a big issue locally, mobile phone masts going up – that kind of discussion of local issues and those things that affect people as local residents. We've just taken over the Neighbourhood Watch because we do hear gossip intrinsically, events that are going on, we are a conduit for information whether it's to and from, whether it's from the police, the local neighbourhood, local residents. Advertising local events. There's a local choral group who meet*

> *here. There's events on in the local churches and we keep programmes for local theatres and cinemas so people can find out what's going on. We have collection boxes and so on to raise money especially for local charities. We get phone calls literally once or twice a week saying can you do this, that or the other....'* **Landlady, rural pub, Hertfordshire**

Another told us:

> *'We do a lot of work with the local church. You hear a lot of bad things about pubs in the papers – corruption of the young and so on – but pubs are about community. The vicar works behind the bar once a year. We have sponsored walks and a music festival.'* **Landlord, rural pub, Gloucestershire**

It is estimated that the average pub raises around £3,000 a year for charitable causes, although this is probably below the average for community pubs. Punch Taverns has calculated that its pubs raise on average of £3,369 a year each for charity, which amounts to £120 million each year (APPBG 2008).

Public services

In rural areas in particular, community pubs are becoming the host for a range of important public services on which local residents depend. At the more informal end the regular pub community can provide an important network of social support, with people able to borrow things from one another, look out for one another and even get advice and counselling over a quiet beer:

> *'There's a bloke who comes into this pub who is 87 years old – he's been drinking in this pub since Bobby's dad ran the pub – pre-war – he comes down on his little scooter thing – if Wendy or Bob don't see him or if any of the drinking community don't hear from him, someone will always be monitoring where he is.'* **Man, village pub, Cambridgeshire**

> *'We're all customers – they've got a business to run. But we ain't just customers, we're friends. If I needed something, he'd help me out. Wendy I'll confide things to. That's what makes a pub.'* **Man, village pub, Cambridgeshire**

> *'We do community activities of various kinds. There was a village newsletter sponsored by Help the Aged which we now produce. We provide an inter-village post – people bring their Christmas cards down here and people can pick them up. We have a notice board for people to advertise their trade. We keep stuff for the neighbours when they are not in. We do a discounted meal for the OAPs on a Thursday.'* **Landlord, village pub, Essex**

Pubs also act as places where people can find out about local trade and where business takes place:

> 'The other thing is for local tradesmen and business people, they connect with each other, there's a lot of discussion of business issues. And when people are looking for tradesmen, quite often we get asked, do you know, can you recommend a such and such? Between us and between the customers themselves.' **Landlady, rural pub, Hertfordshire**

> 'It's actually a bit of a business centre as well. There are people who are in here who can get linked with a job or buying a property, you can interact in that way.' **Man, inner city pub, Hackney**

More formally, a number of pubs, particularly in rural areas, are delivering important public services, such as running the local shop, taking over a threatened local post office or providing access to broadband internet. The 'Pub is the Hub' scheme is a volunteer-run organisation that for the last seven years has encouraged rural pubs to diversify, such as through co-locating services, and supports hundreds of such schemes around the country (see Box 3.1). These can help preserve vital local amenities, but also tend to increase footfall through the pub and help keep it viable.

> 'We've run the post office from a spare room for the last six or seven years. We were spared the axe. It's separate from the pub and is generally used by the older people. Financially, we don't depend on it. But it's there if we needed it.' **Landlord, village pub, County Durham**

> 'It's the main meeting place – we're a small village, everyone knows each other. The younger ones come in to use the computer because we don't get good broadband up here.' **Landlady, village pub, Yorkshire Dales**

While diversification is important, one licensee insisted that a pub should always remember that its primary purpose is to facilitate social drinking:

> 'Basically, people just want to come in and have a drink – it is a centre for the community – but you don't want to have to trip over post offices and bike repair works to get into the pub. It's still important for a pub to be a pub.' **Landlord, village pub, Gloucester**

Box 3.1. The 'Pub is the Hub' scheme

Pub is the Hub was set up in 2001 through Business in the Community's Rural Action Programme (launched by HRH the Prince of Wales). It encourages breweries, pub owners, licensees and local communities to work together to help retain and enhance rural services in isolated rural areas and support rural pubs. It does this by finding ways in which pubs can diversify their offer and increase their social and community role.

Additional services that can be provided through village pubs have included:

- Better provision of food and drink: This is the core skill of the licensee and their staff. Sometimes simply changing the offering and the style of food and drink can turn around the viability of the pub.

- Additional retail uses: Many post offices and village stores have closed. Pub is the Hub has strong working relationships with the Post Office and Spar Convenience Stores to help to provide additional outlets for their goods and services.

- Additional facilities: There are many ways to improve the usage and viability of pubs. Examples include:

  − Church services
  − Parish/local club and society meeting place
  − Local pensioner meal support operation
  − Pharmacy collection point
  − Dry cleaning and laundry deposit and collection point
  − Provision of a crèche facility
  − Delivery point for goods bought online
  − Fitness/small gym facility
  − Art and craft gallery
  − Outlet for farm produce or other locally produced goods.

Source: www.pubisthehub.org.uk

Cultural value

Pubs – or at least pubs with certain kinds of characteristics – are felt by many people to have a cultural as well as a practical community value. This is because the traditional community pub is felt to offer certain things that are becoming rare in a society being shaped by global commercial pressures.

Running through much writing about pubs are the twin themes of national identity and loss: the idea that a traditional British institution is under threat. Reflections on the state of the British pub combine a peculiar but culturally resonant mix of small 'c' conservatism (the preference for tradition and continuity and an opposition to 'modernisation') and anti-capitalism (an opposition to the 'McDonaldisation' of the pub, the rise of the big chains, associated with globalisation and big commercial interests) (see, for example, Hutt 1973, Boston 1975 and Kingsnorth 2008).

Related themes emerged strongly in our three focus groups held with pub regulars. It must be said at the outset that these focus groups took place in fairly traditional community pubs and the participants were mostly middle-aged and male. Therefore, their views cannot be taken as representative of the pub-going population as a whole, never mind those people who do not visit pubs regularly. However, the strength of feeling expressed in these groups about the loss of the traditional pub was striking and is worthy of reflection in this report.

First, these pub-goers clearly felt that their pubs offered something traditional – a continuity with and a connection to the past that has value and is felt to be under threat more widely. These participants felt that too many pubs were being 'modernised' by breweries and pub companies, making them too similar to each other.

> *'I grew up in the '70s and '80s and I still think this holds a tradition of being a friendly, down to earth sort of pub, none of this unfriendly bar staff and minimalist décor and chemical beer.'* **Man, inner-city pub, Hackney**

> *'It's an organic, battle train of a place…the floor will be done eventually. In another fifty years.'* *'And as long as we can keep the property developers away.'* **Two men, inner city pub, Hackney**

> *'It's a bit of a fifties throwback…which means that it hasn't been contaminated by the thinking of the brewers and their stupid idiotic interior designers and bloody marketing arseholes.'* **Man, village pub, Cambridgeshire**

> *'It hasn't been "improved".'* **Woman, village pub, Cambridgeshire**

> *'It's still old England, with old fashioned values and old fashioned quality.'* **Man, village pub, Cambridgeshire**

This traditional quality also lends the pub an authenticity which these participants valued – the traditional community pub has developed from the bottom up, as opposed to being designed by people with no connection to the local area beyond a commercial interest in the local drinks market.

We know that commercial motives tend to drive towards standardisation, as we have seen with the rise of so-called 'clone towns' (New Economics Foundation 2006). Whatever its causes, it is a trend that the pub regulars we spoke to did not like.

> *'Most of the pubs that I go to have something slightly unusual about them, slightly quirky, might be for the beer or there's a pub down the road where the landlord is a real character and he does good beer as well, and another one that does good food. But there's a fourth pub that I used to drink in – a Young's pub – it was interesting, the landlord had been there forever, a little bit tatty, a little bit of a boozer. They went in there and got rid of the landlord. Made the place over with sofas and laminate floors and music and they've just taken the "right, this is what we're going to do to all our pubs", apply the marketing model that comes out of headquarters. And you go down any high street and they're all the same, we're just destroying the uniqueness. That's just symptomatic of our country – "giving people what they want".'* **Man, rural pub, Hertfordshire**

> *'They're stripping things of character.'* **Man, rural pub, Hertfordshire**

> *'Wetherspoons try very hard to be accommodating and all that, but it just don't work – it's like drinking in a bloody McDonalds or something.'* **Man, inner-city pub, Hackney**

An important driver behind this sense of authenticity is the fact that the licensees of all three of these pubs were local people, who owned the pub independently.

> *'[I like the pub because it is] owned by the people who live here, who live above it.'* **Man, village pub Cambridgeshire**

Three men in the inner-city pub in Hackney told us they liked the fact that the pub is: *'independent'*; free from *'corporate fucking strategists'* and *'brewery-stroke-hotel management companies'*, and the fact that *'the gov's in charge'*.

One further connected theme that emerged from the focus groups was the idea that the pub represented one last shelter from the changes of the modern world. The traditional community pub is seen as a bastion, a last redoubt:

> *'People do like the older feel to a pub anyway. If it was all metallic and glass model bar, that's not what we want. This is a bastion – and we want to keep it.'* **Man, inner-city pub, Hackney**

> *'This pub from a local point of view is the last bastion.'* **Man, village pub, Cambridgeshire**

This importance of the pub as representing something authentic and traditional runs alongside a hostility among drinkers of real ale[2] to the standardisation and 'gassing up' of beer and the loss of regional breweries. For example:

> *'There's a conspiracy of the big breweries to ensure consistency – if you take a pint of beer and it's delicious – then put gas in it and it'll ruin it … years ago you could go into a pub and if you see a pump at the bar, you were virtually guaranteed a decent pint of beer. But not any more – I've walked out of pubs when I've seen this white rise of disappointment rise up. I'm not drinking that, I won't accept it.'* **Man, rural pub, Hertfordshire**

One response to these concerns is to say that many people choose to drink in chain pubs, wine bars and gastro-pubs with modern interiors. If traditional pubs are in decline, this is because people are not drinking in them. However, the focus groups make clear that there is value in having diversity in our drinking places. There is clearly a constituency for a certain type of traditional pub – rooted in the community through the licensee, with its own organic design and décor, independently owned, retaining important inherited characteristics from its past. The combination of the ownership of the majority of pubs by a handful of large pub companies alongside the commercial pressures to achieve high-volume sales through standardisation means that a significant group of consumers risk losing something that they value and that is important for their quality of life.

Conclusion

This chapter has shown that pubs matter to our communities in various ways. They act as hubs through which local social networks can be strengthened and expanded. Pubs generate more jobs and more government revenues per litre of beer than beer sold in shops and supermarkets. While town centre bars and a small minority of badly run pubs can cause problems of alcohol-related disorder, the vast majority cause no such problems. If anything, it is preferable that people should drink in the controlled environment provided by a pub. While they remain biased towards men, younger people and people with higher disposable incomes, pubs are nevertheless an important local social institution for encouraging people to mix with others from different backgrounds to their own. They enrich local civic life by hosting meetings of local clubs and associations and promoting local charities and events. They directly provide a range of local public services, from the informal social support to members of the drinking community to the provision of post offices and village shops in rural areas.

Community pubs of a certain type also have a cultural value: they represent something authentic and traditional in the face of powerful commercial and market pressures towards standardisation and 'clone pubs'.

---

2. This term was coined by CAMRA in the early 1970s to differentiate between the big brewers' processed beers and beers brewed using traditional ingredients and left to mature in the cask from which they are served in the pub through a process called secondary fermentation.

4. Time for change

This report has so far made two arguments: first, community pubs are working within increasingly tight margins and are closing at historically high rates. Second, these pub closures do not simply affect licensees but have a wide social impact, too.

This chapter asks what needs to change if we are to put these community pubs on a sounder footing and give them a chance to succeed.

The case for change

Government is not to blame for all the problems facing community pubs. The industry itself needs to change and in particular the relationship between the pubcos and their tenants needs reform. There is also a great deal that pubs can do themselves to try to get through this recession, through diversifying what they are offering prospective customers.

Nor is it the job of government to support businesses that are selling products people no longer wish to buy.

However, the policy framework as it currently stands is hindering rather than helping community pubs. There are three main flaws with the current approach:

- The current policy framework is far too indiscriminate. Rightly, the Government is concerned with reducing crime and promoting public health. However, in order to do this it has increased alcohol duties and brought in new regulations that, because of the size of their operations, have hit community pubs harder than the town centre bars that are most associated with the problems caused by excessive drinking. We need a more nuanced approach that targets the 'problem' drinking places and rewards and incentivises pubs that play a positive role in their communities.

- The policy framework is counter-productive. By making beer through the 'on-trade' channel more expensive, while allowing it to be undercut through discounted sales in the off-trade, we are encouraging more people to drink, often excessively, outside the controlled environment of the pub. Furthermore, beer sold through the off-trade generates less tax revenue and creates fewer jobs than beer sold in pubs. In these ways the policy framework runs directly counter to important public policy objectives.

- Policy fails to recognise that very many pubs are more than just businesses, but also perform important community functions which if lost can have a serious impact on the quality of local community life. The community pub therefore requires greater recognition in legislative and policy terms as an important local amenity.

Recommendations

The following recommendations aim to provide greater support for the majority of well-run community pubs that bring so many of the benefits described in this report and that are currently struggling.

Business rate relief for 'centres of community'

Pubs currently pay business rates like any other business, in a way that does not recognise the wider community role they play. Some pubs can benefit from rural rate relief of 50 per cent if they are the last pub in the village and they have a rateable value of under £10,500. There is an additional discretionary relief that a local authority can make available to such rural pubs where they are felt to benefit the community.

There is no reason why this should not apply to urban and suburban pubs as well, given the community contribution that we know many of them make. Indeed, rather then just refer to public houses, the Government could introduce mandatory 50 per cent business rate relief for any business that also acts as a 'centre of community'. This would help those pubs that perform the vital community functions we have described and also creates an incentive for other pubs to expand their local community role. Box 4.1 sets out the criteria such a centre of community would have to meet.

Box 4.1. Recommended criteria for business rate relief for a centre of community

There should be a mandatory 50 per cent rate relief for a premises occupied by a business that is also a centre of community.

A centre of community should fulfil all of the following criteria. It should:

- be a place in which local social networks are significantly strengthened and extended
- be a place in which people from different backgrounds mix and socialise to a significant extent
- provide important local public services, such as a post office, general store, internet access, a pharmacy collection point or free use of its toilet facilities
- have regular charitable fundraising taking place on its premises
- be used for meetings of local groups (for example, sports, cultural, political, business and voluntary groups)
- not cause significant problems of noise nuisance or crime, as certified by the Environmental Health department and the local police.

The extent to which these criteria are met can be measured using the Social Return on Investment (SROI) methodology set out in Appendix C to this report. The research for the SROI study should be carried out by the licensee and local community according to Department for Communities and Local Government guidelines. Mandatory relief should be granted by the local authority where the SROI research clearly establishes the business as a centre of community.

Eligibility for third-sector finance to develop the community-oriented side of the pub business

We have argued that many pubs are not just retailers but also make an important community contribution.

This raises the issue of why such pubs should not be able to apply for third-sector grants or loans. For example, the Government's 'Future Builders' scheme provides grants and loans to third-sector organisations to help them further develop their services and businesses (charities, voluntary organisations, social enterprises, industrial or provident societies or community interest companies). The Community Builders fund provides finance to expand multi-purpose community-led organisations that provide a similar 'community anchor' role to that performed by many community pubs.

This should not require any change to policy because pubs could under current rules apply to become Community Interest Companies (CICs), which are eligible for some third-sector funding. This is a new legal entity established by the Government to promote social enterprise (see Box 4.2 for details). It might be an attractive model for community pubs because it recognises that they are businesses rather than charities, allowing profits to be made, but also ensuring there is an overriding community benefit as well. It might be particularly attractive in cases where local people step in to buy their local pub to prevent its loss – in other words where the primary motivation is not to make money, but rather to retain a community institution.

Appendix C of this report shows how community pubs might be able to measure in monetary terms their wider social impact, using the Social Return on Investment methodology. This tool should help community pubs demonstrate their wider social impact, which will be critical in successfully applying for third-sector funding.

Box 4.2. Community Interest Companies

Community Interest Companies are limited by shares or guarantee, which are allowed to pay dividends to their shareholders and make profits, but which must also operate in the interest of the community.

Their community orientation is in part secured through the 'asset lock' mechanism, which means that the firm's assets and profits have to be either retained within the CIC or transferred to another asset-locked organisation. This ensures they cannot be sold on for private profit and must be retained for community benefit.

Community Interest Companies are monitored by a national CIC Regulator. There are currently over 800 CICs operating in the UK.

Source: www.cicregulator.gov.uk

Reform planning law to protect community pubs

For years communities have struggled to prevent their local pubs closing so that the owner can sell the land for housing. In 1999 the Government changed planning guidance to ensure that where there is only one pub left in a village, it should not be granted a change of use until its viability as a pub has been properly tested by an independent valuer. Planning Policy Statement 7, which covers development in rural areas, requires local authorities to adopt development policies supporting the retention of community facilities including rural public houses. However, Planning Policy Statement 6 does not impose a similar obligation to protect urban and suburban pubs.

The status of community pubs as local amenities needs to be strengthened in planning law to prevent viable pubs being lost:

- Planning guidance should require local authorities to adopt policies to support the retention of important community facilities, including public houses, in urban and rural areas.

- A mandatory viability test should be met prior to any application to change the use of the property from a public house to some other class of use. The CAMRA Public House Viability Test provides a model for this, setting out a number of key criteria for establishing viability including, for example, the potential local market, the existing competition and local transport links.

- The Government should close the loophole in the current law that allows developers to demolish a pub without permission for a change of use and then apply for a new use for a new building on the same site. This allows developers to bypass the existing protections and should be brought to an end.

In the absence of nationwide reform, some of these proposals could be brought about in individual local authorities by using the 2007 Sustainable Communities Act. This Act sets up a process by which councils can drive government action. It gives councils the power to make proposals to the Secretary of State as to how government can 'assist councils in promoting the sustainability of local communities'. The Secretary of State is then under a duty to 'reach agreement' with councils, via their representative body, the Local Government Association (LGA) on which proposals are given priority. The Act defines local sustainability as 'encouraging the economic, social and environmental well being of the authority's area'. For example, local authorities could ask for the power to make planning policy stronger to sustain public houses as important community facilities.

Ban the use of restricted covenants

It has become apparent that some pub companies are putting in place restricted covenants upon the sale of their pubs that prevent a property being used as a pub in the future. This practice should be banned.

A tenant's right to buy

We know that the longevity of a licensee is critical to the success of any community pub. Our focus groups found that pub regulars like their pubs to be run by a person who lives locally and sees the pub as providing an important service to the community. We also know that the longevity of the licensee is critical in keeping any aggravation or trouble under control (Marsh and Fox Kibby 1992).

However, often pub companies or breweries sell pubs in clusters, giving existing tenants no opportunity to buy the pub. To prevent the loss of long-standing licensees from community pubs, when a pub is sold the existing tenant or lessee should be given the first option of buying it at open market valuation.

Minimum pricing to reduce the price differential between the 'on' and the 'off' trade

The difference between the price of beer sold in the on and the off trades has led to more people drinking at home or in places other than licensed premises. As beer tax has increased, so too has the price of beer in pubs. The supermarkets are able to use their market power to ensure that increased duty is not passed on by their suppliers. They can also afford to sell alcohol at below cost and as a loss leader to entice customers through their doors and spend on other products.

Alcohol is not like any old commodity, because excessive consumption is damaging to health and contributes significantly to crime and disorder. This is why alcohol is taxed in the first place. There is therefore a case for preventing the sale of alcohol at very low prices. To do this a minimum retail price per unit of alcohol should be introduced.

The Scottish Government has recently published plans to implement such a policy and the Chief Medical Officer has argued that the rest of the country should follow suit. Researchers at Sheffield University estimate that a minimum price of 40p per unit would reduce consumption especially among excessive drinkers and the young. While this would put up prices in shops and supermarkets, pub prices are already well above that level and would be unaffected. The policy could therefore help to close the price differential between the off and on trades, as well as ending irresponsible promotions (Scottish Government 2009).

A freeze on beer duty

Given the above-inflationary increases in beer taxation in recent years and given the state of the pubs trade, the Government should abandon plans for a beer duty escalator and maintain beer taxation at its current level. This should help prevent the price differential between the off and on trades getting any wider.

Re-balancing the relationship between pubcos and their tenants

We have argued that the current policy framework is failing. However, pub closures cannot be laid at the Government's door only – there is a great deal the industry itself needs to do to ensure the viability and sustainability of community pubs.

There is evidence that the beer tie and in some cases rent increases by pub companies have prevented otherwise viable pubs from succeeding. Opinion polls show licensees to be very concerned about the impact of the tie on their ability to compete. As the economy has turned sour it is the leased estates of the large pub companies that are struggling the most, compared with the managed chains like Wetherspoons, which can offer discounts on food and drink. Tied tenants are unable to compete by dropping their prices to bring people through the door. This is not good for the tenants, nor for consumers, as these pubs are unable to respond flexibly to consumer demand. The Business and Enterprise Committee is continuing to examine these questions but it is clear that this is an area ripe for reform.

The beer tie

It is clear that the tie as it is being operated at the moment by some of the pub companies does limit the ability of tenants to compete effectively, by keeping their beer prices high.

Scrapping the beer tie altogether would be a radical step – similar in magnitude to the 1989 Beer Orders, which had a number of unforeseen consequences. Abolishing the beer tie is something of a 'Pandora's Box': we believe there is enough evidence to show that the beer tie is causing serious problems for many tenants but we do not yet know whether abolishing it altogether might create another set of equally troubling problems.

There are a number of concerns about abolishing the tie altogether:

- The pub companies might simply sell large swathes of their estates, leading to even more pub closures.
- Scrapping the tie might harm the regional brewers because they depend on their tied estate to get their beers to local markets.
- The pub companies might simply increase their 'dry rents' to compensate for the loss in 'wet rent'.
- It is unclear whether smaller pubs with relatively low barrelage would be able to extract significant discounts from the breweries.

Given these concerns, the Government should instigate an urgent review of the beer tie as it is currently operated. It should refer the whole question of the tie to the Office of Fair Trading (OFT) to consider independently whether or not the way the tie as currently being operated is fair. The Government should also consider the following options for reform:

- Forcing the pubcos to publish data on the amount of discounts forgone for each of their pubs, strengthening the negotiating hand of the tenants.
- Including the money the pubcos are making from those discounts in the overall rent calculation. Tenants could then claim part of the discounts which

are not currently being passed on. Incorporated into the rent calculation, this could then be subject to independent arbitration to ensure tenants got a fair price for their beer.

- Allowing tenants to buy in guest beers, out of their tie. This would force the pubcos to offer tenants a competitive price for their beer, given that they would have to compete with sales of the guest beers from outside the tie.
- Capping the number of pubs that any single company can own, to increase tenants' choice and reduce the dominance of the large pubcos.

Rents

The question of the fairness and transparency of pubco rents should be dealt with by bringing in a mandatory code of conduct across the industry. The 2004 Trade and Industry Select Committee gave the industry the opportunity to reform through a voluntary code, but it is clear that bad practice continues.

A mandatory code of conduct would ensure that rents are calculated in a fair and transparent fashion. There should be:

- an end to upward-only rent reviews
- a national framework for the calculation of rents and tenants should be provided with a comprehensive breakdown of how their rents were calculated
- an independent arbitration system to settle disputed rents and this should be subsidised by the pubcos to ensure that it is affordable for tenants.

The machine tie

The 'amusement with prizes' machine tie should be removed. There is no justification in pub companies taking 50 per cent of games profits when the performance of the machines has little to do with them.

Diversification

There is a great deal that pubs can do to diversify and develop their businesses. To the extent that pubs are suffering from changing consumer tastes and lifestyles, they need to change what it is that they are offering.

Many pubs around the country have been doing well by, for example:

- Letting out rooms or setting themselves up as bed-and-breakfasts
- Expanding the range and improving the quality of food they offer
- Putting on a wider range of entertainment
- Focusing on real ale, which can attract an important section of the beer-drinking community; some pubs have even opened up their own micro-breweries
- Providing a wider selection of drinks to appeal beyond the beer-drinking consumer, for example selling a wider range of wines.

As one landlady running a specialist real ale pub told ippr:

> *'None of it is rocket science – so many pubs don't focus on real ale. They focus on music, on food, on parties, on numbers because it's a big place. Pubs are diversifying – and those that are successful will be those that do whatever it is that they do very well – whether it's beer or music or food or whatever. The bigger pubs that are trying to please all the people all the time – they'll struggle because you end up not doing anything very well.'* **Landlady, rural pub, Hertfordshire**

To support the pub trade in diversifying, the Government should:

* consider providing funding to the Pub is the Hub, which is voluntarily run and provides advice and support for pubs in rural areas seeking to diversify
* close the loophole by which tied pubs are not allowed to apply for loans under the Small Firms Loans Guarantee scheme. This exclusion was originally made on the basis that the breweries would provide loan support to their pubs. But times have changed and tied tenants are now effectively small business people who should be as eligible for such loans as any other small enterprise is.

Training and skills

The pub trade has a weak culture of training and professional development. After the initial mandatory licensing qualification there is no requirement for further qualifications and little incentive to take up courses. The professional body for the licensed retail sector, the BII, offers a range of inn-keeping courses but licensees have to pay for them at full cost. The Learning and Skills Council will only give support to people taking much longer courses that are felt to be impractical for people in the pub trade. The BII claims as a consequence that 'the licensed retail sector has been largely disenfranchised from the skills agenda' (APPBG 2008: 38).

The Department for Innovation, Universities and Skills should therefore explore ways in which the licensed trade could be integrated into current systems of support for training and professional development. Improved training should also help counteract the extent to which community pubs suffer from alcohol-related disorder given that 45 per cent of alcohol-related disorder in pubs is due to poor management. Although the Government's proposal for mandatory training for all bar staff has not been well received in the industry on cost grounds, it is in the industry's long-term interests to ensure that it does what it can to promote responsible drinking. Training is critical to that and the Government is right to insist on it.

Conclusion

There is no magic bullet that will transform the fortunes of Britain's community pubs overnight. This chapter has set out a range of reforms to the current policy framework that as a package give greater recognition to the fact that local pubs are often more than just businesses, but also provide an important community service as well.

5. Conclusion

It is widely believed that over the last thirty years we have become a more private and individualistic society. Policymakers across the western world are rightly concerned about the social consequences of populations who increasingly stay at home, keep themselves to themselves and become disengaged from their surrounding communities. While supporting community pubs will not on its own reverse such trends, doing so should form part of any wider agenda aimed at raising levels of social capital and fostering better connected, more vibrant local neighbourhoods.

This report has shown that community pubs are more than just private businesses selling alcohol. They are also in many cases community hubs, offering a space where local people can meet and socialise – as one of our interviewees described it, 'a place where a community can bounce off itself'. They are perceived by the public to be an important place where people from different backgrounds can meet and interact. They provide a meeting place for a whole myriad of local community groups and in some cases provide important public services, such as by supporting local post offices and general stores that might otherwise disappear.

There is no magic bullet that will reverse the accelerating rate of pub closures. Some people argue that the closures are entirely the Government's fault, while others point the finger at the large pub companies. The truth, as ever, is more complicated than that and this report has argued that we need to take a broader approach if we are to support community pubs in the years ahead.

From government we need a more nuanced policy framework that focuses support on well-run community pubs and creates incentives for others to play an active role in their communities. We need greater recognition in policy terms that pubs are often more than just businesses, meriting greater protection from property developers and more support from the tax system. Greater support from government should be matched by serious reform to the way the industry currently operates, so that viable community pubs are not put out of business because of excessively high rents or beer prices.

If all this is done there is no reason why the community pub, one of our oldest and most popular social institutions, should not continue to open its doors and play a role in local community life for many generations to come.

References

All Party Parliamentary Beer Group (APPBG) (2008) *Community Pub Inquiry* London: All Party Parliamentary Beer Group

BBC News online (2007) 'New restaurants hits record high', 15 August, available at http://news.bbc.co.uk/1/hi/england/london/6947340.stm

Boston R (1975) *Beer and Skittles* Glasgow: William Collins Sons & Co. Ltd.

British Beer and Pub Association (BBPA) (2008a) *Statistical Handbook. A compilation of drinks industry statistics* London: Brewing Publications Ltd.

British Beer and Pub Association (BBPA) (2008b) *A Wake Up for Westminster. Economic trends in the beer and pub sector* London: BBPA

British Beer and Pub Association (BBPA) (2009) BBPA website, various pages, available at www.beerandpub.com

Burke T (2006) *The English Inn* London: Read Books

Business and Enterprise Committee (2009) *Uncorrected Transcript of Oral Evidence To be published as HC 26-i*, available at www.publications.parliament.uk/pa/cm200809/cmselect/cmberr/uc26-i/uc02602.htm

CGA Strategy (2009a) 'Drinks Places', web page available at www.cgastrategy.co.uk/products/drinksplaces.shtml

CGA Strategy (2009b) 'Analysis of pubs by constituency (England, Scotland, Wales only)' Unpublished

Communities and Local Government (CLG) (2007) 'Indices of Deprivation 2007', web page, available at www.communities.gov.uk/communities/ neighbourhoodrenewal/deprivation/deprivation07/

Davis B (1981) *The Traditional English Pub. A Way of Drinking* London: The Architectural Press

Department of Health (2008) *Smoke free England – One Year On* London: DoH, available at www.smokefreeengland.co.uk/files/dhs01_01-one-year-on-report-final.pdf

Ernst and Young (2007) *The Contribution Made by Beer to the British Economy* Amsterdam: Ernst and Young

Financial Times, The (2009a) 'Punch shares suffer sales woes',14 January

Financial Times, The (2009b) 'Wetherspoon scraps dividend to meet debt', 20 January

Financial Times, The (2009c) 'Enterprise rallies despite bleak update', 22 January

Financial Times, The (2009d) 'Resilient sales put Greene King in the pink', 29 January

Financial Times, The (2009e) 'Growth brings post-Christmas cheer to pub groups', 30 January

Fox K (1996) *Passport to the Pub. The Tourist's Guide to Pub Etiquette* London: Brewers and Licensed Retailers Association

Haydon P (1994) *The English Pub. A History* London: Robert Hale Ltd.

Home Office (2009) 'Alcohol related crime', web page, available at www.homeoffice.gov.uk/crime-victims/reducing-crime/alcohol-related-crime/

House of Commons Trade and Industry Select Committee (2004) *Pub Companies. Second Report of Session 2004-2005* London: House of Commons

Hutt C (1973) *The Death of the English Pub* London: Arrow

Independent, The (2007) 'Cinema attendances hits highest level for 38 years', 28 September, available at www.independent.co.uk/arts-entertainment/films/news/cinema-attendances-hit-highest-level-for-38-years-464771.html

Independent, The (2009) 'The Footsie Failures', 4 March, available at www.independent.co.uk/news/business/analysis-and-features/the-footsie-failures-1637020.html

Indices of Multiple Deprivation (2007) *Indices of Multiple Deprivation* London: Communities and Local Government

Jennings P (2007) *The Local. A History of the English Pub* Gloucestershire: The History Press Ltd.

Kingsnorth P (2008) *Real England. The Battle Against the Bland* London: Portobello Books Ltd.

Marsh P and Fox Kibby K (1992) *Drinking and Public Disorder* Oxford: MCM Research

Mass Observation (1943) *The Pub and the People. A Worktown Study* London: Victor Gollancz

MCM Research (1990) *Conflict and violence in pubs* Oxford: MCM Research

Mintel (2008) *The Impact of the Smoking Ban* London: Mintel. Summary available at www.marketresearchworld.net/index.php?option=com_content&task=view&id=1770&Itemid=77

Morning Advertiser (2009) 'Leased pubs value gap passed tipping point', 29 January

New Economics Foundation (NEF) (2006) *Clone Town Britain. The survey results on the bland state of the nation* London: NEF

New Economics Foundation (NEF) (2007) *Measuring Value. A guide to Social Return On Investment* London: NEF

NHS Information Centre for Health and Social Care (2008) *Healthy Lifestyle Behaviours: Model Based Estimates, 2003-2005* London: National Centre for Social Research and The NHS Information Centre for Health and Social Care

Observer, The (2008) 'Public smoking ban hits pubs' beer sales', 6 July, available at www.guardian.co.uk/business/2008/jul/06/fooddrinks.retail

Publican, The (2008) 'Beer Tie Opposition Mounts', 25 September, available at www.thepublican.com/story.asp?storycode=61257

Rollo J, Lewis V and Borius A (2008) *Industry View In-Line: Leisure and Hotels. Leased Pubs – Avoid* London: Morgan Stanley

Scottish Government (2009) *Changing Scotland's Relationship with Alcohol. A framework for action* Edinburgh: Scottish Government

Sky News online (2007) 'Pubs want to keep smoking ban', 29 October, available at http://news.sky.com/skynews/Home/Sky-News-Archive/Article/20080641290517

Social Issues Research Centre (SIRC) (2002) *Counting the cost. The measurement and recording of alcohol-related crime and disorder* London: The Portman Group

Social Issues Research Centre (SIRC) (2008) *The Enduring Appeal of the Local. Report of research conducted by the Social Issues Research Centre* Oxford: SIRC

Travers T, Tunstall R and Whitehead C with Pruvot S (2007) *Population mobility and service provision. A report for London Councils* London: LSE available at www.londoncouncils.gov.uk/upload/public/attachments/997/LSE %20Population %20Mobility %20report %20- %20Feb %202007.pdf

Appendix A: Interviews

ippr conducted interviews with the following people during the course of this research. The interviews mainly took place by telephone between December 2008 and March 2009, although some took place in person.

Licensees in the following pubs:

- Estate pub, Hackney (pubco tied)
- Village pub, County Durham (freehouse)
- Rural food-led pub, Somerset
- Rural pub, Derbyshire (tied, pubco)
- Village pub, Lancashire (tied, brewery-owned managed house)
- Village pub, North Yorkshire (tied, brewery)
- Village pub, Essex (freehouse)
- Rural pub, Hertfordshire (freehouse)
- Village pub, Cumbria (freehouse)
- Rural pub, Gloucestershire (freehouse)
- Rural pub, Cornwall (freehouse)
- Two urban pubs, South London (one pubco tied, one non-tied)
- Urban pub, Central London (pubco tied)
- Urban pub, Newcastle upon Tyne (pubco tied)
- Village pub, Cambridgeshire (freehouse)
- Village pub, Hertfordshire (community-owned freehouse)
- Village pub, Berkshire (community-owned freehouse)
- Rural pub, Lincolnshire (parish-council-owned freehouse)
- Rural pub, Macclesfield (pubco tied)
- Village pub, Cambridgeshire (freehouse)

Interviews were also conducted with:

- Greg Mulholland MP, All Party Parliamentary Save Our Pubs Group
- Community pub activist, Cambridgeshire
- Mike Benner, chief executive, CAMRA
- Jonathan Mail, head of policy and public affairs, CAMRA
- Tony Payne, chief executive, Federation of Licensed Victualler's Associations

Appendix B: Focus groups

Three focus groups were conducted during the course of this research, with the following participants:

Inner city pub, Hackney, December 2008

- Elderly white male
- Middle-aged Asian male
- Three middle-aged white males

Rural pub, Hertfordshire, January 2009

- Five middle-aged white males
- Two middle-aged white women
- One young white man

Village pub, Cambridgeshire, January 2009

- One middle-aged white woman
- Four middle-aged white males

Appendix C: Method for measuring the social value of a community pub

Social Return on Investment (SROI)

SROI is a way of understanding, measuring and reporting the social, environmental and economic value that is created by an organisation. It captures social value by translating social objectives into financial and non-financial measures.

SROI was originally pioneered by the Roberts Enterprise Development Fund, a San Francisco-based venture philanthropy fund. It has since been taken up internationally and has been developed further in the UK by the New Economics Foundation (NEF) and the SROI Network. It has now been highlighted by the UK's Office of the Third Sector as a research tool that can be used by not-for-profit organisations to demonstrate their impact.

This section goes through the SROI methodology and shows how it could be applied in the case of a community pub. By explaining the method in some detail this section should be helpful for licensees, community groups or brewers and pubcos wanting to prove their pub's social impact.

The method

There are three main stages to the SROI method and in what follows we apply these to develop a way of measuring the social impact of a community pub. Note that we have simplified the method to make it more straightforward and we have removed those steps that did not seem relevant to the community pub sector. For the full detailed methodology readers should consult the New Economics Foundation guide to SROI (NEF 2007).

Stage 1: Boundary setting and impact mapping

Step 1: Establish the parameters
The first step is to scope out the impact the pub is believed to have on the local community. This will help us decide which things we want to measure. For example, this might include the impact of the pub on local social networks, employment or the provision of public services, such as supporting a local shop or post office.

Step 2: Identify stakeholders
In order to measure the impact of a pub we need to develop a list of those people or organisations that affect or are affected by the pub's activities – its stakeholders.

For example, for the average community pub this might include regular pub-goers, the wider residential community and the local clubs and societies that use the pub for their meetings. We must also decide which stakeholders are most important and prioritise those in the analysis.

Step 3. Develop an impact map

The impact map sets out a 'theory of change' – in other words the cause and effect relationships that explain how the pub affects its local environment. This should contain a number of key elements:

- Inputs: the resources put into the pub by the licensee, the pub owner, the staff and customers
- Activities: the things that happen in the pub that those resources contribute towards
- Outputs: the direct results of those activities
- Outcomes: the longer-term or more significant results of those activities
- Impact: those outcomes that the pub itself can take credit for.

Note that we should include both negative and positive outputs and outcomes: for example, in the case of a pub we should assess whether it has had a negative or positive effect on community cohesion, on crime or on noise nuisance.

In assessing the impact of the pub we also need to account for those things that might have happened regardless of whether the pub was there or not: this is done by considering attribution, deadweight and displacement:

- *Attribution* is the process by which we explain which outcomes directly resulted from the pub's activities, as opposed to the activities of another organisation or group of people. For example, how do we know that it was our local pub, as opposed to another pub or social club, that helped strengthen social networks in the local area?
- *Deadweight* is the process by which we exclude those outcomes that would have occurred anyway: for example, because of the presence of other community hubs like community centres or community cafes that perform similar functions.
- *Displacement* is the process by which the positive activities of one organisation may crowd out those of another, thus having a nil overall impact. For example, this would be the case if the opening of a successful new community pub led to the closure of another similar such pub down the road.

An example impact map for a community pub is set out in Table A.1 below. This is just an example of what such a map might look like – the maps of individual pubs will of course differ depending on their circumstances and their particular activities.

Table A.1. A community pub impact map

Stakeholder	Input	Activity	Output	Outcome	Impact
Pub-goers	Money	Socialising	Met new people	Extended social networks	Taken into account attribution, deadweight and displacement
		Participation in charity fundraisers	Met people from different backgrounds	Enhanced community cohesion	
		Witnessed a fight in the pub	Spent time with friends or family	Strengthened existing social networks	
			Raised money for charity	Promoted local good causes	
			Personal insecurity	Increased fear of crime and disorder in the community	
Wider residential community	Money Time	Visited post office situated in pub	Purchase of postal services, raising revenue for licensee	Supported local economic activity and employment	Taken into account attribution, deadweight and displacement
		Use function room for community meetings	Meetings held which help local groups function	Supported access to public services locally	
		Experienced noise nuisance late at night	Sleep frequently disturbed	Improved level of civic activity	
				Loss of peace and quiet in neighbourhood	
Licensee	Skills Time Money	Provided food and drink for sale	Raised income, made profit	Sustained pub	Taken into account attribution, deadweight and displacement
		Hired local staff and paid for local goods and services	Increased local employment	Contributed to local economy	